Practical History Teaching

Alan Jamieson

Evans Brothers Limited London

Published by Evans Brothers Limited
Montague House, Russell Square, London, W.C.1

First published 1971

SBN 237 28515 0   PRA 2721
Phototypeset by Filmtype Services Ltd., Scarborough
Printed and Bound in Great Britain by
T. & A. Constable Ltd., Edinburgh

Contents

Acknowledgements

The author and publishers are indebted to the following for permission to reproduce copyright material in this book:

D. S. Daniell and George G. Harrap & Co., Ltd., for the quotation from 'Cap of Honour: the story of the Gloucestershire regiment'.
A. D. Peters & Company for the quotation from 'The Adventures of John Wetherell' by C. S. Forester.
Mr. Brian Smith, Gloucester Record Office. The Trustees of the British Museum. Gloucestershire County Council. The National Maritime Museum. The Illustrated London News and Sketch, Ltd. The Essex Record Office. Lord Sherborne. Rodborough Parish Council. Pictorial Education. Geffrye Museum, London. London Museum. City Museum, Bristol. The Science Museum. Aerofilms Ltd. Leigh Parish Council. Miss Eugenie Alexander. Art and Craft in Education. Archives photographiques, Paris. The Post Office.

Illustrations

Preface

The idea of writing this book arose out of a number of courses given to students and serving teachers. The practical activities for children incorporate schemes prepared for and tried out in primary and secondary schools. The book is also something of a cry of desperation to teachers of history to examine their objectives and their methods.

History is on the defensive and it is becoming more and more difficult to justify the continuation of school history where formal traditional methods of teaching prevail. Fortunately, the generation is now passing that believed it to be one's duty to send young teachers into schools equipped with files of neat notes conscientiously copied from books and lectures and repeated in examinations. These notes were then condensed for their pupils, who in turn passed examinations, went on to college and university and returned to school to repeat the whole wearying process. The great fault of this business was that facts were conveyed from one generation to another without the exercise of brain or imagination. Indeed, this dull routine spread the belief that history was a fixed package of knowledge to be passed intact from generation to generation. Those who succumbed to this persuasive view forgot the true nature of history, that it is ever-changing and that each new generation views past events in a different light. 'History is, or ought to be, the least authoritarian of the sciences', wrote V. H. Galbraith. 'Its essential value lies in the shock and excitement aroused by the impact of the very ways of thought of the past upon the mind.' Too few youngsters feel this excitement, this stirring of the mind and the imagination. This book provides examples of areas where children can share in these experiences by learning for themselves, where they can burrow for their history and record it in various ways, where they might explore books and places of historical interest and so learn from their own practical activities.

Deliberately, there is no place here for a discussion of technological aids: films, filmstrips, the tape recorder, overhead projector, record-player, television and radio. These are valuable tools for the history teacher, but they do not enter into the catalogue of practical activities. The film and the tape still assume a passive audience, unless children are to make their own films and recordings: advice on that subject is beyond my knowledge. The practical schemes outlined in this book are being employed now in schools or have been tried out by teachers and lecturers.

The book is written for teachers of history and students who are about to become teachers of history. For convenience, the terms 'masters', 'boys' and 'his' have been used: this is not to exclude the history taught by ladies to ladies. The activities referred to are designed for pupils in the junior-secondary range, that is between the ages of 9 and 13, and one hopes that primary and secondary school teachers will find something of practical value in these schemes. The pupils considered here are those of average ability. Plato's wise advice is particularly appropriate for these children: 'Knowledge which is acquired under compulsion obtains no hold on the mind. So do not use compulsion but let early education be a sort of amusement.'

Chapter One   Traditional Methods: Soliloquy and Lament

In recent years history teaching in schools has come under severe and sustained attack. The main assault criticises the dullness of teaching methods and the irrelevance of the content of school history. These accusations have arisen for a number of reasons and it is perhaps pertinent to enquire briefly into them here. The pressure of external examinations, the lack of initiative in developing varied methods of teaching, the reluctance of teachers to abandon the chronological 'development of western civilisation' syllabus, and the failure to keep pace with the rapid developments in educational technology have all played their part in pushing history into the doldrums. As the writers of the Newsom Report asserted: 'Geography and perhaps even more frequently history lessons are expendable as far as boys, and to a less extent girls are concerned. They cannot buy anything with this kind of knowledge as they can with physics and shorthand; they are not always willing to pay for it with hard work as they will for the skills of handicraft or dressmaking. Henry Ford's "History is bunk", did they but know it, expresses exactly what they feel; but, of course, Henry Ford is as dead to them as Queen Anne – or History'.[1]

Teachers can only answer this taunt if they are sure that history is serving a valid educational purpose. Is it developing attitudes and giving children experiences which might enable them to understand something of the adult world they are about to enter? Is it helping to train minds, to present opportunities to weigh evidence, make judgements and develop skills? Does it allow children to express their opinions and ideas in varied forms? Many educationalists who are not historians would be reluctant to give an

[1] Newsom Report: *Half Our Future*, p. 163.

affirmative answer to these questions. Many would simply say 'No'.

History is in the melting-pot. Its very existence is threatened by such monsters of the deep as 'Social Studies', 'Integrated Studies' and other *avant-garde* subjects. Increasingly, headmasters and headmistresses are finding that when more time is demanded by the mathematicians, scientists and sociologists, it is history which is squeezed out of the timetable, and it is history which provides them with the justification for doing so. Lack of relevance to the modern world; the remoteness of history from children's lives and experiences; dull teaching (deadened by the repetition of notes, which is a particularly baleful influence) – these are some of the criticisms that one hears all too often. 'In no other subject is there so much teaching and so little learning' wrote the editors of *The Teaching of History* (IAAM, 1965) glumly. The challenge is clear. Unless teachers rapidly reconsider objectives, content and methods, history will disappear from schools or become, like Classics, the interest of a small and declining number of pupils.

The number of books and articles produced in recent years telling history teachers how to do their job is legion, and one hesitates before adding to this number. Some of these exhortations are listed at the end of this chapter. However, one does notice that there are far fewer books which make practical suggestions on methods of teaching, with practical examples to illustrate the theme. This book does not provide an instant, successful answer, but it does suggest some approaches which might bring the answer to the class teacher. Too much school history is dull because it is given in the form of stereotyped, ready-packaged goods, with little opportunity for the use of imagination and initiative by children, who enjoy and respond to varied methods of teaching. Children welcome the chance to work things out for themselves, to write their own history. In the past, school history has suffered from an excess of dull, inactive teaching. It is time to put this right.

Raison d'être

A full discussion of the philosophy of teaching history in schools is not relevant to this book. If anyone wishes to follow a discussion on these lines, W. H. Burston provides a thoughtful and stimulating introduction in *Principles of History Teaching*. However, if we are to deal adequately with content and method, a brief note should be added to define the objectives that lie behind such methods, and if we are to persuade teachers to vary their approaches and to risk trying new ground, it is necessary to justify the bargaining position.

The major factor in deciding the content of history in schools, and ultimately therefore in deciding methods, is the ability and interests of the pupils we teach. The antagonism and suspicion with which 'educationalists' are regarded in staff common rooms arise from the schoolteacher's reluctance to relate 'the child' referred to in the textbook with that young barbarian Bloggs or chirpy little Emily in the corner of the classroom. The teacher will be more prepared to adopt new schemes if a practical suggestion can readily be applied to the children under his care: conversely, he will be suspicious of a writer talking of 'children' in general.

If we start, then, from the viewpoint of the child and not of the subject, history can help to realise three important educational aims: that of enabling children to understand something of the community and the society in which they live; that of developing skills such as oral and written communication; and, by reading, writing, acting and other activities, that of helping children to understand themselves.

History is a subject that appeals to children of all ages and all mental abilities. It is not difficult to arouse enthusiasm in a class with a story about Joan of Arc, the Charge of the Light Brigade or the Battle of Jutland. A constantly changing audience enjoys stories about real men. Children appreciate action and movement, the expression of emotions and feelings, adventure, ambition and travel. A story of people struggling to attain worthwhile objectives, and the perils which they

faced and overcame can be inspiring for any age. Very often, action and adventure loom large. 'Castles', 'the Vikings', 'the Norman Conquest' and the 'Crusades' seem to provide the staple diet of a good many history lessons in primary schools. Not surprisingly, teachers give children what they appear to want – absorbing stories about people in dangerous situations.

Of course, this is not all that history has to offer; but it is one answer to the difficult problem of making the world of adults comprehensible to children. The motivations that determine human action are often too complex for children to understand and yet our pupils do struggle to master the details of what men did in the past, even if they cannot grasp why they did them. This, though, is vitally important to historical thinking, that pupils should try to understand the motives and the actions of others by an imaginative transference to another place and another time. If children carry over this sympathy for other people, and are able to appreciate how others felt and acted in given situations, they are developing feelings that will help them as adults. But this is largely supposition, and in practice, history teaching falls far short of such ideals.

The attempts to substitute 'people' for individuals in civics or social studies have failed, because 'people' is an abstraction that does not seem to appeal to children. They can appreciate the problems of a Henry VIII or Richard Chancellor, but not of 'the middle class' or even of 'the poor'. Equally, constitutional and political history have failed to make much impact: they are too remote and prosaic to kindle enthusiasm, unless they are translated into personal terms.

But history is not just about individuals in the past. It deals with changes in society and man's attempt to control and exploit his environment. If history can help children to understand something of these processes of living and working in a community, and at the same time can satisfy a natural curiosity about the past, it is serving a useful social purpose. Unfortunately, too little actual classroom teaching seems to be related to these objectives. Children have a great capacity for imaginative work, indeed a far greater capacity than many teachers would admit. Yet history teachers are slow to offer this insight into events and people in the past. Too much time is spent on essay-writing, note-taking and note-making. Information that is discovered, examined and recorded by children themselves is likely to have far more impact than facts that are provided, ready-made, by a conscientious tutor. If the only sources of information are the teacher and the textbook, pupils come to think of history as something which exists only in books or in the depths of the teacher's mind. On the other hand, a large number of other sources and methods of inquiry can help children to become aware of different views and the variety of historical evidence.

What do we teach?

There is no simple answer to this complex question. How can there be when the size and nature of schools differ so radically one from another, and the abilities of children vary so greatly? The teacher in the primary school or the junior forms of the secondary school considers himself fortunate if he has two thirty-minute periods a week per form for his subject. In the middle years of the secondary school, history very often becomes an 'option' alongside music or chemistry. Some children will therefore be studying history until they are thirteen, and others until they are eighteen. How does one measure the intellectual abilities of children, when such demands of time and compression exist?

Moreover, teachers are constantly being advised to find a place for 'contemporary' history, for American, Chinese or Russian history, for 20th-century world history and local history. These are some of the factors that determine syllabus construction, and beyond them there are the beckoning spectres of GCE and CSE. In framing a syllabus to meet these considerations, one must be ruthless and relentless. Obviously, one has to select from the great mass of material, and preferably on the basis of the objectives set out in the early part of this chapter. Many traditional topics retain their place largely out of teachers' loyalty to lost causes. Do the Stuarts have to cling to the coat-tails of the Tudors? Why do some ninety per cent of secondary schools begin their courses with Greek and Roman history? Is there any reason for continuing to teach subjects such as the Magna Carta, Petition of Right and Palmerston's foreign policy to children whose understanding of such subjects will be extremely limited?

Assuming that one starts planning a syllabus with a blank sheet, there are two important questions which must immediately be answered:

does the course have to follow a chronological pattern, and is it going to be an outline of the history of western civilisation? It is a rare and daring teacher who says 'no' to both questions. The average primary and secondary school course follows one of the two patterns set out below:

A Year 1 Early civilisations
    Year 2 English History to 1485
    Year 3 Tudors and Stuarts
    Year 4 19th and 20th century Britain and Europe

B Year 1 English History to 1485
    Year 2 Tudors and Stuarts
    Year 3 18th century
    Year 4 19th and 20th century Britain and Europe

One finds that the great mass of textbooks has followed this pattern too. indeed, one is inclined to say that supply has on occasions dictated demand. The advocates of the traditional syllabus resist change by arguing that it gives a 'sound knowledge of history, a love of history and an introduction to the understanding of history'.[1]

As early as 1926 the Hadow Committee saw the danger of overloading the syllabus. It noted the difficulty, 'in the amount of material that it is possible to present'. However, schools had their clear duty: 'to ensure that no large factor should be entirely omitted . . . the whole period, at least from the time of the Romans to the present, should be covered in some form'.[2] Similarly, L. W. Cowie, writing nearly forty years later in the Handbook for History Teachers, was equally adamant: 'The normal history syllabus, therefore, proceeds steadily during the four years of the secondary school from the beginning of recorded time, the theme which gives it unity being the growth of western civilisation.' And this indigestible fare does not allow for any tampering: 'It is a mistake to suppose that there are different sorts of history to be taught to children of varying intellectual ability.'[3]

Unfortunately, the refrain is repeated in the primary school. R. J. Unstead, the doyen in this field, after asserting that 'junior children have

[1] I.A.A.M., The Teaching of History. CUP, 3rd edition, 1965 p. 15.
[2] Report of the Consultative Committee on The Education of the Adolescent, 1927, pp. 199–200.
[3] W. H. Burston and C. W. Green (editors), Handbook for History Teachers. Methuen, 1962.

no chronological sense', goes on to suggest a four-year course running from Early Man to Victoria.

The faults of the outline chronological syllabus for all but the most swift and skilful minds have often been debated. The hectic gallop through the centuries, once in the primary school and then again in the secondary school, has little to commend it. Superficiality, an excess of oral teaching, the consequent limitations on children's activities, the inevitable tide of fact upon fact – these are some of the sad and unavoidable consequences. Faced with the pressure of completing this advance from the mastodon to Mussolini, teachers fall back on oral teaching, describing and explaining as they proceed, while the class obediently listens and answers the occasional question. The Socratic method of questioning is very difficult to maintain when children have little knowledge of the subject under discussion, and teaching of this type simply develops into monologue. The pupils play secondary roles: they are the recipients of information chosen and arranged by the teacher. Children cannot be given the opportunity to explore for themselves, to go off on tangents: there simply is 'no time'. Little reflection, deduction and imagination are necessary to sit through this type of lesson.

There is a place for a certain amount of oral teaching in all subjects, including history. The danger lies in overdoing it, in cramming facts into neat, packaged units, often by means of dictated notes. The obvious inability of the great majority of children to absorb this mass of fact year after year must bring this approach very near to total failure with a large percentage of the school population.

Faced by the hostility of children to this type of teaching, many schoolmasters have tried alternative forms of syllabus construction. One of these alternatives is the 'line of development', which takes a horizontal slice from history. Themes rather than periods are studied – communications and transport, agriculture, industry, local history, home life through the ages, the development of the colonies and so on. The champion of this approach has been Professor M. V. C. Jeffreys, and his influence can be seen in some of the schemes proposed by CSE boards. Whatever its drawbacks, the idea does at least permit some flexibility, and it does throw more of the initiative on to the shoulders of children. By studying topics, less able children can often realise a greater sense of purpose than in an outlines course. The great defect of this approach is that pupils who study transport, costume or warfare through the ages as topics in themselves are not likely to gain much insight into any one age as a whole. They might understand a great deal about the many methods of using the wheel but they are not likely to acquire an understanding of life in the Middle Ages or in Tudor or Victorian Britain.[1]

Another alternative is the 'patch' system. Instead of an outline, the teacher selects a number of periods of history and the class, working as individuals or in groups, study aspects of the age. In this way one can spend a full term on Elizabethan England rather than chasing all the Tudors in this time. The patch does allow study in depth, and aspects of an age, such as architectural changes or contemporary literature, which are not normally examined in an outline course, can be dealt with. The system also allows for project work and more varied forms of children's activities, largely because the pace is more leisurely and children have time to read topic books and even to sit back and reflect.

The 'era' approach selects even more rigorously: one or two eras in each century are examined in turn. Teaching by topics incorporates the ideas of both the patch and the line of development, and has been attempted most successfully in other subjects in primary schools. Most enterprising teachers have adopted or adapted all these different systems to their own teaching. For example, within an outline course on the Middle Ages it is possible to examine one era in a little more depth; to take a number of topics – monasteries, castles, roads, the village, – and study them more thoroughly. It is possible to follow the line of warfare through five centuries at the same time.

None of these systems has really replaced the traditional chronological survey. Despite their uncertainties and forebodings, most history teachers cling to the outlines syllabus; this is the consequence of their dissatisfaction with the alternatives added to a feeling that their duty to make pupils informed about history can be achieved only through the traditional forms.

[1] There is a short and apposite discussion on the comparative values of the line of development, patch, era and outline methods of syllabus construction in *History for the Average Child*, by P. H. J. Gosden and D. W. Sylvester, Blackwell, 1968.

Modus operandi

Most of the criticism levelled against history teaching in schools deals not so much with the content of the subject but with the methods by which it is taught. In 1952 the writers of the booklet *Teaching History* asserted that one of the objectives in the study of history was to give children an 'imaginative experience'. Furthermore, 'to embrace it properly a quality of sympathetic imagination is needed, a humility about one's own age and the things to which one is accustomed, a willingness to enter into a different experience'.[1] Does history teaching in primary and secondary schools give the pupils sufficient opportunities for this exercise of the imagination?

Note-making and note-giving still play too prominent a part in history teaching. History is not merely the recording of information in notebooks, but if it is to be anything more than this, teachers will need to intensify their efforts to make the subject interesting and vivid. The story of the Crusades is a lively, exciting topic. If lessons on the subject are leaden, and children are inattentive and learn with difficulty, the fault lies surely not with the Crusades but with the teacher. With the freedom that exists in British education, the choice of content and method lies almost entirely in the teachers' hands. Within the bounds of timetable and finance, they have a free choice. And yet, despite this freedom, history teaching languishes. It suffers too much from the dead learning that A. N. Whitehead has warned us against: 'inert ideas which have no bearing on a child's natural activities of body or mind, and do nothing to illuminate or guide his experience'.[2]

Again, as with the content of history lessons, there is no magical, revolutionary answer. But there are approaches to teaching which might bring the individual teacher closer to his answer. In many schools there are brilliant teachers, capturing the interest and the imagination of their pupils with vivid teaching. There is always the place for the exciting story, the lucid account, the dramatic recapitulation of a battle or the joy of a discovery. Unfortunately, for every good storyteller there are dozens of poor ones, and, in addition many children cannot concentrate for more than ten minutes on oral teaching.

Perhaps the greatest fault in history teaching

[1] *Teaching History.* HMSO, 1952, p. 17.
[2] A. N. Whitehead. *The Aims of Education.* Benn, 2nd edition, 1950.

is too great a reliance on mere talk. We must devise methods of involving children more actively in history. Children will respond, if given the chance, to the opportunity to use more than one book, consult more than one reference, to model, act, visit places of historical interest, to handle photocopies of documents and to study local history. Above all, children are willing to make their own judgements, conduct their own researches and record and analyse material in varied forms – if they are given the opportunity.

The psychologists of the Piaget school tell us that children between the ages of nine and thirteen are still in the stage of 'concrete operational thinking'. This means that they deal largely in the real and the present and can reason only from materials which they can see, touch and use. The forms of adult thinking that we take for granted: the ability to draw contrasts; to relate events in one historical age to events in another; to analyse consequences, and to deal in concepts such as tyranny, revolution, constitution, socialism – these skills are still largely dormant. But children of this age can appreciate time; they can recognise the succession of events; they can understand that ways of life in earlier civilisations were different from ours; they can follow a story and reason from evidence. These children are capable of discovering information for themselves, of making judgements and formulating opinions based on evidence, and of expressing their own thoughts and ideas in various practical forms. This is where history can play a part, by enlisting and developing these capabilities.

Many teachers would agree, even if they are not convinced by Piaget, that children learn more easily and more effectively if they can grapple with and solve problems on their own terms. Much of the disillusionment regarding history in schools has stemmed from the apparent rejection of this approach. Instead, children are apparently still being spoon-fed with information and inert ideas. 'Write down the causes of the Hundred Years' War from these notes on the blackboard', or 'Summarise the achievements of Gladstone in his first Ministry' are, unfortunately, all too often the instructions one hears in many secondary schools.

One wishes that more teachers would vary their approach to the recording of information and would devise schemes by which children can investigate problems, collect information and assess results from evidence that is available in other places apart from the blackboard and the textbook. In the same way, more opportunities for self-expression might be offered through writing, drawing, painting, acting and modelling.

As children grow older, their interest in men's motives and in cause and effect grows, so that it becomes possible in the middle and upper forms of a secondary school to analyse history in a little more depth. At this stage, children begin to think more about the world outside school and about their own careers. They often challenge history's relevance to this beckoning world, and are reluctant to project themselves back into the past as they did in the primary school and the lower forms of the secondary school.

Thus, at a time when the power of reasoned thought and greater mastery of expression are developing, children often turn away from both the content and the methods of history that gripped them at an earlier stage of personal development. This tragedy faces not only the historians but teachers of other subjects. However, one must admit that the scientists, mathematicians and English specialists have risen to the challenge more enthusiastically and effectively, often assisted by the Schools Council, the Nuffield Foundation and other bodies. Is there some magical elixir that will transform history into a dynamic, attractive subject? There are as many different answers to that question as there are history teachers. But one answer is variety, for this is one ingredient that has been sadly lacking. Varied methods, with a large proportion of time devoted to practical, active learning, will not bring Utopia overnight but might save history from oblivion.

Some teachers might question these assertions on the grounds that unless children are prepared to read, teachers can accomplish little. History is about the past and its subject-matter lies largely in books. This is true, and the reluctance to read is very sad; but this is not an insuperable difficulty. There are other skills which children can bring to the history lesson. At all events, history does have the great advantage that no basic structure, as with mathematics, and no set of formal rules, as with languages, have to be learned before work can begin. Children who can read, write, act, build up visual illustrations in various materials, model in a number of different substances and contribute with a spade or a camera to fieldwork can study history in their own way and in their own time.

Practical history

When the era, patch, line of development and other systems of studying history fail, the reason is mainly that they still begin with 'history', with the content and not the consumers. If any 'revolution' in history teaching is to take place, it has to begin with children and their methods of learning, not with the syllabus. Within reason, depending on age and ability, almost any period of history is suitable for study in the classroom. If one is dealing with the Romans, for instance, the sixth form might be able to assess the legacy of Roman law and government, but a primary class will concentrate on roads, camps and the story of Julius Agricola. The criterion is not one of period, but one of selection of teaching material relevant to age and ability.

This is all rather obvious, but it is remarkable how many teachers select their material from the viewpoint of history rather than that of children. However, to involve children more effectively in the learning process, which is the point of this book, rigorous and relentless selection of material is necessary. If one wants children to learn for themselves through individual or group work, the conventional syllabus must be done away with. Pupils will not be satisfied with superficial treatment: they want to explore in depth, and this cannot be done without sacrifices.

Probably the best type of syllabus which allows for the discovery of information, varies the means of expressing ideas and recording information, and gives time for reading is one which takes a series of patches within an outlines course and abandons everything else. For instance, if a year's course is 'The Middle Ages', one would select topics within this time-scale and allow pupils to work through them. Some of these topics might be the Conquest, the Church, medieval warfare, the Crusades, the medieval town and so on – topics which contain stories, biographical details, opportunities for children's work and also convey the essence of the period.

This is not to say that history in schools is to be undisciplined. Like every other branch of knowledge, open-ended learning often leads to boredom and dead ends. Children's learning must be directed for it to be effective: the teacher's role changes, but it is no less essential. Questions have still to be put, work schemes to be planned and directed. However, if children are to be allowed to express their own ideas in many different forms, the teacher must be flexible, both in his control of a class and his expectations of the ground to be covered. If the teacher has the determination to follow through these methods of teaching, he will discover that three important skills are developed along the way: an understanding of how to search for information, the ability to interpret it, and the awareness of how to express it.

To select material that is useful for a specific purpose, to arrive at conclusions of one's own based on evidence, to plan and execute methods of expressing opinions and facts in various forms – these are ambitious objectives in education. While teachers still cling to the chronological endurance race, children rarely have the opportunity to explore these possibilities until the sixth form, and then another spectre, public examinations, prevents the squandering of time that such methods might involve. History can play a part in training these skills, but until the teacher is brave enough to abandon traditional syllabuses and methods, he is unlikely to make a contribution to these developments.

The objective of 'practical' or 'active' history is to involve children, mentally and physically, in learning situations. This could of course apply to a class reading quietly. They are involved and active. On the other hand, there are many children who cannot read quietly for long periods and for them more flexible and varied methods are necessary. Ideally, one would like children to examine source material, search for information, form judgements based on what they discover and express their opinions in different ways. If this can be achieved through drama, illustration (painting, drawing, modelling, photography), work-cards and work-books, visits, the construction of scrapbooks and class displays and the use of the library and documents, history teachers can feel that they are restoring the tarnished reputation of history and are giving many children an opportunity to enjoy a subject that they might have rejected, had it been taught in a formal manner. There are difficulties and dangers, and many of these problems are dealt with in the following chapters, but if they can be overcome, the habits of research and independent thought that ought to come from activity methods is both the children's and the teachers' reward.

Some reference books on the teaching of history

Barraclough G., *History in a Changing World*, Blackwell, 1956

Bell J. J., *History in Schools*, Wheaton, 1945

Burston W. H., *Principles of History Teaching*, Methuen, 1963

Burston W. H. and Green C. W., *A Handbook for History Teachers*, Methuen, 1962

Burston W. H. and Thompson D., *Studies in the Nature and Teaching of History*, Routledge, 1967

Carpenter P., *History Teaching: the Era Approach*, CUP, 1964

Collingwood R. G., *The Idea of History*, OUP, 1946

Dance E. H., *History the Betrayer: A Study of Bias*, Hutchinson, 1960

Dwyer F. J., *The Teaching of History in Secondary Schools*, Historical Association, 1964

Fairley J. A., *Activity Methods in History*, Nelson, 1967

Finberg H. P. R. (editor), *Approaches to History*, Routledge, 1962

Gardiner P., *The Nature of Historical Explanation*, OUP, 1952

Happold F. C., *The Approach to History*, Christophers, 1950

Hill C. P., *Suggestions on the Teaching of History*, UNESCO, 1953

I.A.A.M., *The Teaching of History*, 3rd edition, CUP, 1965

Jeffreys M. V. C., *History in Schools: The Study of Development*, Pitman, 1939

Johnson H., *The Teaching of History in Elementary and Secondary Schools*, Macmillan, (New York), 1940

Lewis E. M., *Teaching History in Secondary Schools*, Evans, 1960

Milliken E. and Milliken E. K., *Handwork Methods in the Teaching of History*, Wheaton, rev. edition, 1960

Ministry of Education, Department of Education and Science, Pamphlet No. 23 *The Teaching of History*, HMSO, 1952; Pamphlet No. 52 *Towards World History*, HMSO, 1967; Pamphlet No. 54 *Archives and Education*, HMSO, 1968

Renier G. J., *History: its Purpose and Method*, Allen and Unwin, 1950

Rowse A. L., *The Use of History*, Hodder, 1946

Sharpe J. T., *The Teaching of History in Primary Schools*, Macmillan, 1961

Strong C. F., *History in the Primary School*, ULP, 1950

Strong C. F., *History in the Secondary School*, ULP, 1958

Unstead R. J., *Teaching History in the Junior School*, A & C Black, 2nd edition, 1959

Walsh W. H., *An Introduction to Philosophy of History*, Hutchinson, 1951

Chapter Two   Projects in the Classroom

There is nothing very new or revolutionary about project work. However, enthusiasm for this method of teaching has grown increasingly in recent years. The dissatisfaction felt by many teachers at the excessive use of 'talk and chalk' methods has led to the desire to experiment with an approach that involves children more directly in the learning process. Teachers who have not rationalised their behaviour or methods in this way have nevertheless gone over to projects almost out of desperation in the face of bored and obstreperous children. At the very least children can be kept occupied by projects: the depressing sight of rows of uninterested and inattentive faces can be immediately banished. However, one hopes that project work has far more value than simply as a means of keeping children quiet. Projects have immense value in giving children the opportunity to discover knowledge for themselves, instead of having it presented like a dead fish on a silver salver.

One of the earlier forms of project work was the Dalton Plan. This scheme envisaged the almost complete disappearance of the separation of the school timetable into periods: instead, teachers directed individual and class investigations into topics that cut across both timetable and subject divisions. A paler but effective imitation of this method of classroom organisation, free from the often claustrophobic atmosphere of subject teachers, has been adopted in many primary schools. In junior schools one sees a great deal of class and individual work on topics such as farming, villages, food, transport and industry – topics in which history, geography, science and English can be combined. In this way, history becomes one of a number of disciplines, and the subject divisions which are often the bane of many secondary schools disappear entirely from the school curriculum.

What the Dalton Plan, topics and projects have in common is a desire to break away from conventional methods towards a more child-centred classroom organisation, where pupils do their own ferreting for information, form their own opinions and record and express their work in varied forms. There is a very full discussion of the objectives and methods of project work in primary schools by Peter Rance in *Teaching by Topics* (Ward Lock Educational, 1968). Rance distinguishes between environmental studies, topics and projects, and shows how all these varying means of organisation can cut across the traditional curricular subjects. Sheila Ferguson, on the other hand, in *Projects in History* (Batsford, 1967), adapts projects to one subject, history, and makes many practical and useful suggestions on content and organisation.

Project work in primary and secondary schools can be organised along various lines: some of the most effective and proven methods are outlined here.

1. Individual projects within a general class theme. Supposing that the work for the term was to be concerned with medieval Britain, each child could be given a topic, such as transport, houses, dress, food, armour, weapons, the monasteries, the tournament, the town, farming and so on. By using classbooks and library books, children would write their own accounts, draw or paint pictures, paste illustrations into their scrapbooks, and finally report their achievements to the rest of the class so that the information they have unearthed may be shared. This can also be done by preparing folders which are passed around the class for other children to read.

One of the dangers and, at the same time, one

of the strengths of project work is that children become specialists in only one aspect of history. They might acquire a detailed knowledge of medieval siege warfare or the wool trade, but have understood little of the broad picture of medieval society. However, this criticism is surely secondary to the superior objective, suggested in the Newsom Report, of gaining 'something in depth for a short time rather than a little of everything all the time'. In terms of child participation, insight and understanding, the child gains far more by a personal examination in depth of one aspect of the age than he does by a mad gallop over the centuries.

2. Another type of project may be carried out through group work, where classes are divided into groups of three, four or five children, who explore a topic and present their work to the class either as an exhibition or in oral form. In group work, children can be set more ambitious projects such as model-making, drama or scrapbooks, and their written work can be mounted for class display on wall charts, friezes or folders.

At the completion of several weeks' work, the children ought to have produced a 'book' or folder on the subjects they have chosen to study. This is research work on a simple level, for the children are seeking information for themselves, following up clues that the teacher has laid or that they have discovered for themselves, and writing up the results of their surveys. One has to be careful that pupils do not slavishly copy chunks of ill-digested material from books: this is a great danger and can only be avoided by careful tutoring.

Children at almost all levels of age and ability can be set to work on projects: the advantage is that the slow pupil sets his own pace and the swift worker races on, unimpeded by his more deliberate fellows, to complete one project and carry on to another. Teachers who are dealing with GCE 'O' and 'A' level candidates often look askance at project work. They are foolish to do so, for the method can be adopted to examination work. It is more difficult to eliminate formal teaching in examination preparation work than in any other field of teaching. Fortunately, many CSE panels are experimenting with the project work approach and are finding that children respond to the responsibility of individual initiative more than they do to more stereotyped, formal methods. Even so, children in the upper ranges of the secondary school who are preparing for external examinations total only some eight per cent of the total school population. There is really nothing, therefore, to prevent the use of project work in secondary schools.

3. There are advocates of other methods of organising project teaching – the 'line of development', the 'topic', the 'era' and the 'patch'. Class, group or individual projects can be set within all these forms of organisation. To give some practical examples:

(a) If the *line of development* theme for a month's work was *Ships Through the Ages*, children working in groups or as individuals could study the ships of the Egyptians; the Phoenicians; the Greeks; the Romans; medieval ships; the navy of Henry VIII; Nelson's navy; famous ships – the *Cutty Sark*, the *Victory*, the *Golden Hind*; iron ships; the war at sea 1914–18; life at sea – dress, food, disease; modern ships – the battleship, the submarine, the *Queen Elizabeth II*, adding a dozen alternatives that spring to mind.

(b) If the *topic* for a term was *Transport in the 19th century*, the projects could include railways – Stephenson, Trevithick, the Stockton–Darlington; the railway mania; the navvies; roads – tolls, the post, inns, the stage-coaches, turnpikes; road-building – Macadam, Telford and Metcalf; ships – sailing ships, Brunel and the *Great Eastern*, steamship routes, the East India trade; and the birth of the motor car.

(c) Taking as the unit one *era*, and assuming that one chooses 1900–1914, the projects might be: suffragettes; transport; Lloyd George and the Welfare State; politics; the approach of war; fashions; the motor car; the royal family; home life; social unrest; and so on.

(d) If the *patch* was *medieval Britain*, the projects could well be: monasteries; education; food; church architecture; music; ships; armour; weapons; castles; the tournament; the guilds; the Crusades; Henry II and Becket; and so on.

P. Carpenter, in *History Teaching: The Era Approach* (CUP, 1964), discusses this method of teaching and outlines a number of practical suggestions for the treatment of different ages.

On occasions the class teacher feels that to allow children to choose their own topics and to write long analyses in their own time does not allow him sufficient opportunity to teach subjects that he regards as vitally important. Where do political history, civics, current affairs and contemporary history fit into the picture? The answer to this question is simply that projects can be set within almost any framework by assigning special subjects to individual children.

Or as a compromise with more formal teaching, the teacher could devote one period a week to class teaching on the old lines and another period to projects, on the principle that half a cake is better than none.

A group of students once remarked that project work made the teacher's task comparatively easy. Instead of grinding away at the terms of the 1832 Reform Act, the children rushed about while teacher sat back with the *Times*. Put to work with groups of children, these students swiftly changed their opinions. Projects involve far more exhausting work than class teaching. In the first place, class organisation has to be efficient. Books have to be made available on a number of topics; visual aids have to be found; paints, pencils, model-making materials have to be collected and replenished. Above all, the teacher must expect his class to be noisier. Fortunately, this arises from the bustle of work, with children moving about from desk to book-shelf, from modelling table to the teacher. In short, the methods of the teachers of art and woodwork are transferred in part to the history room. The teacher must also be prepared for immediate consultation on erudite topics, as if he were a walking encyclopaedia. He has to instil enthusiasm, control it when a pupil threatens to write the history of England, and encourage it if keenness wilts. He must be one step ahead of his pupils, so that when a project is 'finished' he can suggest other lines of inquiry, other illustrations, or another project. Here the teacher takes on the rôle of a tutor, guiding rather than directing. There are, of course, the idlers and the dodgers who have to be jogged along, but one might with a certain degree of confident optimism suggest that they will be less in number and less vociferous if the rest of the class are employed on their own concerns.

The rewards for this form of teaching are considerable. The exhaustion at the end of the day is not all one-sided; the children have at least come to grips with the methods of historical research, humble though their contributions might be. A child, instead of being a pail, to be filled, emptied and refilled with a mass of information which he forgets at the first opportunity, digs for himself and guards his knowledge as if it were gold. All this might sound Elysian, but the method works if the teacher is keen and is prepared to wrestle with difficulties. As with local history studies, working from source material or by modelling, history becomes a practical subject. If history can help children to work on their own, to distinguish relevant from irrelevant material, and to act on their own judgement, the educational value of the subject is increased immensely. One might say that this could be true of almost any subject, but practical history has another side to it, for it can give children a feeling for the past and a taste of the colour, life and excitement of past societies.

The teacher cannot expect work of high standard immediately. Children need to be trained to find and assemble information, and therefore the earlier they are given the opportunity for individual work, the more likely they are to achieve results of a worthwhile standard. Far more primary schools than secondary schools tackle projects, and many secondary school teachers might be surprised to find their pupils aware of the methods of research and with some experience of them.

Like every other method, project work can become dulled by over-exposure. One has only to hear the resigned remark from a pupil, 'Oh! not another project', to realise that it is time for a change and that projects can with benefit be forgotten for a term or a year.

Organisation of projects

One of the major difficulties is the choice of subjects. Invariably, girls want to write about costume and boys wish to tackle military topics. Many children find it difficult to decide on a subject and have to be closely guided when they begin work. Ideally, suggestions for topics should be drawn from the pupils themselves, but often a teacher may have to transmit his enthusiasm to an individual. Library books, pictures, a film-strip, an outside visit, a programme or an idea from television or radio, a visit from an outsider (a policeman or nurse) – all these can be used to stimulate ideas. Hobbies, personal interests, links with home and family, future careers, skill in art, drama or craft can also be useful stimuli.

Very often valuable material can be drawn from the home – books, illustrations, diaries and objects. On the other hand, children who are empty of inspiration will accept a dictated suggestion from the teacher and follow it up first with reluctance and then with increasing zest as their interest develops. One would like to divert children from some of the well-worn themes, such as castles and costume, to less-documented subjects, but this can be difficult. As a general rule it is better to describe one local castle than to cover the history of castles, and better to tell the story of the British army in the Crimea than give a general account of warfare.

In organising projects the class teacher must have a plentiful supply of books. Many children are inclined to think that copying from books is all that is needed. They have to be trained to extract information for particular purposes and to read two or three accounts of the same story. As children assemble and arrange information, the teacher should encourage them to phrase accounts in their own words and in their own style. Quotations should be allowed only to illustrate a particular theme or item, by selecting from a contemporary diary or letter: otherwise quoting large sections of books should be frowned upon. Unthinking, slavish copying is worthless, and constitutes one of the chief dangers of project work. Children have to be trained *not* to copy words and sentences which they do not understand. To ensure this, the teacher can issue duplicated sheets of instructions or page references, or give children an entirely free hand. A balance between these extremes might be decided upon, so that children do not copy out irrelevant material.

Writing can begin almost immediately. Children should be encouraged to launch straight into composition, using each new book read as a means of adding to or revising their texts. If children think that they have to read three or four books before they can put pen to paper, projects would never get off the ground. In this way, the teacher can control the scope of the topic by restricting the period of history studied for one child and extending it for another.

The collection of information
Projects are best presented in folders, with material written on loose-leaf sheets of paper. The advantage of this is that additional material can be slipped into place and paintings and illustrations can be added. The folder ought, however, to include far more than written material: maps, pictures, drawings and paintings can all be added. If children are working in groups, it is sensible to have a group-leader who decides on the responsibilities and priorities and who co-ordinates the various contributions.

One should not limit recording work to paper. One group might present their effort as a play, or by dressing dolls in period costume, or by building replicas of a town, building or waterway.

If the 'books' or folders are finished simultaneously (which is not easy to achieve!), they can be passed from one group to another. Alternatively, the books can be used for discussion, with the authors answering questions from the rest of the children. The arrangement of a display of pictures or folders always arouses great interest and some of the written work can be mounted on large sheets of paper and pinned on walls as friezes. The danger here is that projects are sometimes looked upon as a form of window-dressing to impress HMIs, PTAs and stray visitors. Displays are really only useful if they reveal children's work and their understanding of their investigations. This can best be achieved by asking a pupil to describe his work to the rest of his fellows.

There are many practical difficulties in teaching by projects, and one needs to be aware of them. The availability of books is one problem. Ideally, one would like to have one or two copies of a large number of books on different themes, but this can be expensive. A selected list of books and their publishers appears at the end of this chapter. Lack of suitable source material can so easily wreck all one's schemes, but if the expense is too great, one can appeal to the local Schools' Library Service.

Materials for use in projects

In order to break away from excessive oral teaching, it is essential to have other aids in addition to the human voice. Fortunately, the supply and variety of pictorial and written material is increasing. Publishers are more than ever ready to vary the format of school books and to experiment with presentation. Most children need the stimulus of a visual image as much at the secondary as at the primary stage of their education. A picture or an illustrated book can be an effective spur to the imagination, and if a teacher can combine written and pictorial material in his teaching, his pupils will be certain to respond more effectively. However, the sophistication and saturation of modern mass media are such that children may very often cease to observe closely. They can become passive, even casual onlookers. Teachers should, as with books, devise methods of ensuring that children use visual aids by examining them closely, answering questions about them, and using these same materials as stimuli for their own work.

Among the illustrations that are useful in the

classroom are postcards, photographs, illustrated books, historical films, maps, transparencies, slides, charts, filmstrips and wall pictures. All these sources can help to create an atmosphere, stir the imagination and bring the past alive.

Visual material

There is a wide selection of visual material for history teachers. The two essential guidebooks are:

Guide to Illustrative Material for Use in Teaching History, G. A. Williams, Historical Association, 2nd impression, 1965

Visual Aids Catalogue, Part II, The Educational Foundation for Visual Aids (33 Queen Anne Street, London, W.C.1), 1968

The National Union of Teachers publishes *The Treasure Chest for Teachers*, which gives lists of organisations providing teaching material.

There are a number of *periodicals* which are extremely useful for ideas, and other magazines occasionally have pictures that can be cut out and stored for future use.

Pictorial Education, Evans Brothers Limited, Montague House, Russell Square, London, W.C.1, published monthly, has a generous quota of history studies. In April 1970, for instance, there were articles on Canals, Villages, Roman history, the Story of Flight, Composers, legends, the Pilgrim Fathers and Costume.

Visual Education, published monthly by the Educational Foundation for Visual Aids, explains the techniques of using visual material, gives information on courses and publishes relevant articles.

In addition, teachers can take pictures from a large number of publications which contain articles on history or history teaching. Some of the most useful from this point of view are:

History Today, 10 Cannon Street, London, E.C.4.

Teachers World, Evans Brothers Limited, Montague House, Russell Square, London, W.C.1.

The Listener, Broadcasting House, London, W1A 1AA.

The Illustrated London News, 10-16 Elm Street, London, W.C.1.

The Teacher, Derbyshire House, St. Chad's Street, London, W.C.1.

HMSO, 49 High Holborn, London, W.C.1, or available at any of the provincial sales offices. HMSO has a list of pamphlets on castles, abbeys and houses in the care of the Ministry of Public Building and Works – details from Sectional List 27: Ancient Monuments and Historic Buildings.

Copyrights Ltd, 87 Borough High Street, London, S.E.1.

Country Life, 2-10 Tavistock Street, London, W.C.2.

Purnell's histories of *The 20th Century* and of *The Second World War* have superb illustrations.

Knowledge, *Finding Out* and *Look and Learn* are magazines which are popular with children because their format is similar to comics. These educational magazines have useful illustrations and a great deal of valuable information.

The BBC (Publications Department, 35 Marylebone High Street, London, W.1) have wallcharts and pamphlets on current programmes. Old copies of BBC and ITA pamphlets are particularly useful for their pictures, which can be cut out and used on friezes, wall-displays and in scrapbooks.

The National Trust, 42 Queen Anne's Gate, London, S.W.1, has illustrated guide books of the properties in its care.

The illustrated supplements of *The Sunday Times*, the *Observer* and the *Daily Telegraph* are valuable.

Pitkin Pictorials Ltd., 9 John Street, London, W.C.1, produce a series of booklets, *Pride of Britain*, with illustrations.

Teaching aids can also be obtained from the following organisations:

The Historical Association, 59a Kennington Park Road, London, S.E.11, publish pamphlets of general historical interest; a series on the teaching of history (*The Teaching of African History* and *An Introduction to Scottish History*, for instance); a series of *Helps for Students* (*Archaeology for the Historian* and *The Use of Medieval Chronicles*, for example); illustrated booklets, and the magazine, *Teaching History*.

The Central Office of Information, Hercules Road, Westminster Bridge Road, London, S.E.1 (pamphlets).

The Council of Visual Education, 13 Suffolk Street, London, S.W.1

The Commonwealth Institute, South Kensington, London, S.W.7

The Society for Cultural Relations with the USSR, 118 Tottenham Court Road, London, W.1

The United Nations Information Centre, 14 Stratford Place, London, W.1 (UNESCO and other United Nations material, including pictures, wall-charts and films).

The United States of America Information Service, Grosvenor Square, London, W.1

The British Transport Commission, 10 Great College Street, London, S.W.1

The British Insurance Association, Aldermary House, Queen Street, London, E.C.4 (film-strips, booklets and wall-charts).

The British Steel Corporation, Steel House, Tothill Street, London, S.W.1 (films on loan, slides, booklets).

Brooke Bond Education Service, Heathrow House, Bath Road, Cranford, Hounslow, Middlesex (booklets, filmstrips and wall-charts).

Dunlop and Co. Ltd., 10-12 King Street, London, S.W.1 (booklets, films, filmstrips and wall-charts).

Picture books

The picture books published by the Historical Association are in bound covers, but separate pages can easily be detached. There are four books in the series: *The Early Middle Ages*; *The Later Middle Ages*; *Tudor Times*; and *Stuart Times*.

The books edited by Mrs. M. Harrison, *Picture Source Books for Social History* (Allen and Unwin), provide a valuable collection of contemporary illustrations.

At a more humble level there is *The Story of Britain Told in Pictures* (Thomas Hope and Sankey-Hudson Ltd.), and a similar venture, *Picture Reference Books* (Brockhampton Press), which tackles subjects such as *The Elizabethans* and *Railways*.

A magnificent collection of pictures is contained in Macmillan's Class Pictures. There are four groups of 60 pictures in each set, making some 240 pictures in all. Each set has a reference book. Details of these sets can be obtained from Macmillan, Brunel Road, Basingstoke, Hants.

A selection of picture books is given next. The books are suitable for individual and group work on a variety of projects with pupils in the 9 to 13 junior-secondary age and ability ranges.

Batsford, *A History of Everyday Things*, M. and C. H. B. Quennell, Vols. 1-4; S. E. Ellacott, Vol. 5; *Everyday Life in . . .* (*Prehistoric Times, Ancient Rome*, etc.); *Life in . . .* (*Roman Britain, Georgian England*, etc.); *Past into Present* (*Transport*; *Law and Order*); *Junior Heritage* (*Cathedrals*; *Ships*; *Villages*).

Black, *Looking at History*.

Longmans, *Evidence in Pictures*, I. Doncaster (*The Medieval Church*; *Elizabethan Home Life*).

Macmillan, *History Picture Books*; *History in Pictures*.

OUP, *A Picture History of . . .* (*Britain*; *Great Discoveries*); *History in Pictures* (*Homes*; *Furniture*, etc.).

Penguin, *Puffin Picture Books* (*Cathedrals and Churches*; *Historic Houses*).

Studio Vista, *Visual History of Modern Britain*.

Postcards

Teachers can quickly build up their own collection of pictures by collecting postcards. Most galleries, historical sites, buildings and museums have postcards for sale. *The Handbook for History Teachers*, pp. 63-67, gives a list of some of the major museums and galleries which have photographs, illustrated books and postcards for sale, and other lists are contained in the *Guide to Illustrative Material for Use in Teaching History*. Sectional List No. 27, published by HMSO, gives details of the plans and guides to many sites and buildings.

Outside organisations, such as government bodies, private firms, embassies and consulates, are often very generous in providing material. Children enjoy writing to these outside agencies explaining that they are doing some 'research' on a subject and asking for information or illustrations. However, this is a much abused method of acquiring information, most of which is in printed form anyway, and many firms, County Record Officers and museum curators are justifiably irritated by requests (very often from more adult students in universities and colleges of education) for 'all relevant information' on 'turnpikes', 'enclosure' and 'railways', and have stopped playing Lady Bountiful to schools and colleges. Children and students should be warned that unless they ask for specific information, they will be disappointed. However, some public bodies – the BBC, the NCB, the Ministry of Health, the DES, the TUC, city and county councils – are still remarkably generous.

Wall-charts

Wall-charts, made up of pictures, diagrams and information, can usually be made by the teacher. However, collages of pictures with footnotes are becoming more popular with publishers. Many commercial firms produce historical charts, and the *Catalogue of Wall-charts* by the Educational Foundation for Visual Aids gives a clear indication of what is available.

Pictorial Charts Ltd., 181 Uxbridge Road, London, W.7, produce a series of historical wall-charts with notes for the teacher. These are useful, but do not contain work-sheets for children, and it is often difficult to see how these charts can be used except as a wall display. Some of the titles in this series are: The Medieval Village (based on Laxton); Chaucer and the Middle Ages; Shakespeare and his Times; the Renaissance; Great Explorations; Victorian Days; Fashion.

A. Wheaton, Fore Street, Exeter, Devon, produce charts on Architecture (Castles; Churches; Houses); they also have Drama and the Theatre through the Ages, and World History illustrations.

Other publishers and public bodies which produce charts useful for history teachers are:

Geo. Philip and Sons Ltd., 32 Fleet Street, London, E.C.4 (mostly wall-maps).

Ordnance Survey Office, Chessington, Surrey (for large OS archaeological maps).

International Wool Secretariat, 18-20 Regent Street, London, W.1

The Council for Education in World Citizenship, 25 Charles Street, London, W.1

Educational Publications Ltd., East Ardsley, Wakefield, Yorkshire

NCB, Hobart House, Grosvenor Place, London, S.W.1

How are these wall-charts, photographs, postcards and illustrated books best used in the classroom? One can simply pass the illustrations from hand to hand, or fix them to pinboarding as wall displays. But it should be remembered that the material used in this way serves merely as an illustration. Pictures should be linked with individual or group studies as part of the work on a specific theme, with children using illustrations as they do books. Notes can easily be attached to each picture, pointing out special features and asking children to explain various points and to draw their own illustrations. For class teaching, one can obtain a great deal more from the picture if it is projected on to a screen by means of an epidiascope; the teacher can then point out the important details and ask for information and deductions.

Quite often the best pictures that one sees in schools are those made by the teacher on large sheets of white or black paper with pen and ink, paint or chalk. They are often more useful than printed pictures, because they have been designed for a special purpose. For those whose artistic skills do not run to this, a slide or a frame from a filmstrip projected on to a wall or a screen can serve the same purpose.

There are no details here of films and filmstrips. Ideally, in advocating practical methods of teaching history, one should be pressing teachers to construct their own filmstrips or sets of slides. Indeed, many teachers are already doing this. For those who cannot, the *Catalogue of Films and Filmstrips* published by the EFVA, and the list in the *Guide to Illustrative Material for Use in Teaching History* are comprehensive. Logically speaking, children ought to be making their own filmstrips and slides too, and again there is some exciting work being done along these lines in a handful of schools. A filmstrip made by the children of a visit to a castle has a great deal more educational value than a beautifully produced commercial filmstrip. One wishes that more teachers would experiment with photography, but of course the expense and the complicated techniques deter people from such an attempt. However, if the school can afford a camera and a roll of film, a class visit or a group project can easily be illustrated by the children.

Printed books

During the past ten years a torrent of school history books has poured from the presses. Although publishers are still determinedly loyal to the textbook, they are accepting larger numbers of topic and project books for publication. The teacher should aim at having a selection of these books in the school library or on his classroom shelves, so that they are immediately available for class use. If the school or departmental book allowance does not stretch to bulk purchase, the Schools' Library Service will be an essential asset. The traditional method of ordering books still dies hard and one even hears of teachers ordering thirty copies of a single *Jackdaw*. One should aim at having one or two copies of a large number of project books, rather than a large number of copies of one title.

One of the most outstanding contributions to project work has been the *Then and There* series, published by Longmans. This is designed more for the 'patch' approach, but with subjects such as *The Medieval Monastery*, *The Vikings*, *The Motor Revolution* and *Roads and Canals in the 18th century*, they are immediately practicable for project work. Each volume is liberally illustrated, very often with contemporary drawings or engravings.

Some of the series suitable for project work are given below. The titles of the books given in parentheses represent a selection of books from the series.

Allen and Unwin, *Understanding the Modern World* (*Industrial Revolution, Town Life*).

Arnold, *Europe in World History*; *The Story of* . . . (*Ancient Athens*).

Barrie and Rockliff, *New Project Histories*.

Batsford, *Living History* (*Battles and Battlefields*); *Past into Present* (*Home Life*; *Town Life*; *Law and Order*); *Everyday Life*; *Everyday Things*; *Junior Heritage* (*Villages*).

Black, *Looking at History*; *Junior Reference Books* (*Aircraft*; *Roads*); *Social Life in England*.

Blackie, *Know About* . . . (*Crusades*; *Wrecks*); *Topics in Modern History*.

Blackwell, *Exploring History*; *Stories of Britain*; *Time Remembered* (*Invading Britain*); *They Saw it Happen*; *How They Lived*.

Bodley Head, *Study Books* (*Canals*; *Coal*; *Farming*).

Blond, *Town Story*; *Today is History Series* (*Crime and Society*).

Cassell, *Story Behind* . . . ; *Caravel Series*; *History Workshop* (*People and Their Homes*); *Living Through History* (*Homes*; *Villages*).

Chatto and Windus, *Stories of English History* (*The Peasants' Revolt*; *the Armada*); *Young Learner* (*People through the Years*); *Look at the Past*; *Open Your Eyes* (*Man's Forward March*); *Dawn of History*.

Dobson, *The Real Book* (*Highwaymen*; *Pirates*); *Living in England* (*The Elizabethan Age*).

ESA, *How to Explore* (*A Port*; *A Village*); *How Things are Obtained* (*Clothes*; *Roads*); *How Things are Developed* (*Food*; *Castles*).

Evans, *Queensway Histories*; *Visual Histories* (*Tudor Britain*).

Faber, *The Story of* . . . (*The Book*; *Your House*; *The Highway*); *Your Book of* . . . (*Architecture*); *Growing Up in* . . . (*The Norman Conquest*).

Ginn, *History Bookshelves*; *Museum Bookshelves*.

Hamish Hamilton, *History from Familiar Things*; *Look Books* (*Roads*; *Churches*; *The Navy*).

Harrap, *This Wonderful World* (*Inventions*; *Travel through the Ages*).

Hart-Davis, *The Young Historian Books* (*Ancient Greece*).

Heinemann, *History in Action*; *Lives of the People*.

Hulton, *Great Civilisations*.

Johnston and Bacon, *Living in History*.

Longmans, *Then and There*; *Live and Learn* (*Food and Clothes*); *As We Were*; *Focus on History* (*Roman Britain*; *The Plague and the Fire*); *Man's Heritage* (*Clothing and Costume*; *Living in Towns*); *Young Books*; *Modern Times* (*Hitler's Germany*; *Modern China*).

Macmillan, *Sources of History* (*Chartism*); *Social Series* (*About our Town*; *The Post Office at Work*); *History for Today*.

Methuen, *Get to Know*; *Outlines* (*Castles*; *Books*; *Crusades*; *Elizabethan Seamen*).

Muller, *Exploring the Past* (*Finding Out about the Normans*; *Stone Age Britain*); *Junior True Books*; *Let's Look At* . . . (*Houses and Homes*); *True Books* (*The American Civil War*; *The Russian Revolution*).

Murray, *The Changing Shape of Things* (*Transport by Air*).

Nisbet, *What Happened* (*In Feudal England*).

Odhams, *Makers of Britain*.

OUP, *History Through the Ages* (*Home Life*); *How They were Built* (*Bridges*; *Roads*; *Ships*); *Oxford Junior Encyclopaedia*; *People of the Past* (*A Charity School in the 18th century*; *A Romano-British family*); *The Changing World*.

Oliver and Boyd, *The Signpost Library*; *Quest Library*.

Parrish, *They Lived Like This* (*Ancient China*).

Penguin, *Topics in History* (*Alive and Well*).

Phoenix House, *Excursion*.

Rathbone, *The Wonderful World* (*Feast and Famine*; *The Story of the Theatre*).

Routledge, *The How Series* (*Roads*; *Parliament*; *Waterways*); *Local Search Series* (*The English Home*).

University of London Press, *Discovery* (*Houses*; *Costume*; *Railways*).

Ward, *The First Book* (*Egypt*).

Ward Lock, *How Things are Made*; *How Things are Developed*; *How to Explore*.

Warne, *Observer's Books*.

Weidenfeld and Nicolson, *The Young Historian* (*The Renaissance*).

Wheaton, *Read About It*; *Junior Reference Books*; *British Battles Series*.

Biography.
Batsford, *Makers of Britain.*
Bell, *Great Craftsmen.*
Black, *People in History.*
Black, *Lives to Remember.*
Blackie, *Great Endeavour.*
Blackwell, *Who's Who in History*, Vols. 1-4.
Blandford, *Founders of Europe.*
Bodley Head, *Great Men.*
Bodley Head, *Men of the Modern Age.*
Cassell, *Women of Devotion and Courage.*
Cassell, *History Through Great Lives.*
Faber, *Introductory Biographies.*
Faber, *Men and Events.*
Hamish Hamilton, *Six Great . . .* series.
Harrap, *He Went With . . .*
Longmans, *Lives of Achievement.*
Macmillan, *They Served Mankind.*
Methuen, *The Story Biographies; Makers of the Modern World.*
Nelson, *Picture Biographies.*
Newnes, *Men of Speed.*
OUP, *Living Names.*
Wills and Hepworth, (The *Ladybird* series) *Adventures from History.*

Chapter Three   Local History

More than sixty years have elapsed since the study of local history in schools received the recommendation and the blessing of the Board of Education.[1] Since then thousands of teachers in thousands of schools throughout Britain have been freely adapting local history to the classroom. Their cause has been unsung but not unknown. In recent years a number of champions, chief among whom have been Professor Hoskins of the University of Leicester and Mr Robert Douch of the University of Southampton, have shown how local history can be used to enliven and add colour to class teaching and at the same time introduce children to source material. The part played by teachers in running local history societies, archaeological societies and branches of the Historical Association encourage one to think that this common enthusiasm for local history is translated to the classroom. In this chapter, and in another on the use of sources, some practical suggestions are made principally to encourage others to join the growing army of teachers who have found local studies valuable in purging their teaching of what A. N. Whitehead called 'inert ideas'.

The study of local history has a great deal to commend it. In the first place, teachers value local history because it deals with the known – house, village, town and countryside – as distinct from much of national history which contains at least two elements of the unknown – the past and unfamiliar geography. To take only two examples, the history of the medieval town or of the parliamentary enclosure movement can be more effectively taught by reference to local conditions. When the lesson relates to familiar names and

places, and when children have an opportunity to explore the countryside or undertake personal research in the town library, the chances of adding interest and colour to teaching are greatly increased. One can also make history more practical, by visits to sites and museums, by using the facilities of the local record office and libraries, by making models, and by drawing plans and pictures based on personal investigation and observation. In short, children can study people and places that are real to them, which is a welcome alternative to the flaccid and superficial skimming that often accompanies a broader course.

Another advantage of studying local history is that it links the school with the outside world. This arises through visits to local industries, the town hall and government offices, or by studying in depth some aspect of local government, such as the old Poor Law, the office of Mayor, or communications. Finally, there is an opportunity here for children to learn through their own experiences. There is the chance to develop powers of initiative and enquiry, to observe, classify and deduce, largely because there are more varied methods of teaching available, much of which is based on direct observation and analysis.

The opportunities offered by different localities vary enormously, of course. So too do the ages and abilities of children, and class time available for history might be strictly limited. Nevertheless, given the will, it is possible to study local history with children from the age of nine to nineteen. Equally, the range of periods and topics is tremendous. One can take subjects stretching from prehistoric archaeology to the modern town. Some examples might be: Roman Britain; place-names; Christian communities; Danish invasions; the Normans and Domesday; the

[1] The Board of Education *Handbook of Suggestions for the Consideration of Teachers and others concerned in the work of the Public Elementary Schools*, HMSO, 1905.

manor; medieval towns; the village and country life; the guilds; medieval architecture – castles, abbeys and houses; the Reformation; the Civil War; the enclosure movement; the Industrial Revolution; turnpikes; canals; railways; elections; Victorian life – the Poor Law, police, health, education, local government. All these subjects can be used either to illustrate national history or as studies in their own right. Taken together, they give a cross-section of most of the important movements that have changed the face of the towns and the countryside. Naturally, not all these subjects will be covered in every locality and the teacher must expect gaps. In general one would be wise to concentrate on the topics where there is full local treatment – a study of a standard history of the county or city will soon indicate what those topics are, and at the same time reveal a surprising amount of detail concerning them.

To study and teach local history is not easy. Text-books are virtually non-existent, and teachers must be prepared to do a great deal of elementary research themselves. They must also prepare teaching material, visit museums, write questionnaires, arrange for documents to be photocopied and answer a thousand questions on local affairs. The biggest problem is in discovering what printed and documentary material there is and whether it is suitable for children. This problem can only be tackled by visiting the county or city record office and the local libraries. Most libraries have a collection of books on county history, with a catalogue, and the staff of the record office will be able to advise on which documents can be photocopied and used in the classroom. Photocopying is not expensive; a readable copy of a document can be obtained quite cheaply. For a modest outlay, therefore, a school could obtain a set of copies of documents on a theme such as the Poor Law, transport or village life.

For the thoughtful teacher there is another problem which one ought to mention, that of relating local studies to national and international history. There is clearly a danger of concentrating too much on parish pump affairs, so that children fail to look to wider horizons. In the light of this danger, one group of educationists is demanding that children study world history, in order to provide them with some background knowledge of current affairs for their role as world citizens. Another group, however, advocates not the study of Mao's China and de Gaulle's Europe, but the history of Little Piddlington, railways (mostly disused) in Wiltshire or coaching inns in Norfolk, and other similar subjects.

The dangers of parochialism have been so strongly stated in recent years that one feels that teachers will not make the error of teaching local history to the exclusion of the rest of the world.[1] Any answer to this question, if there is an answer, depends on how one approaches the study of history in schools. W. H. Burston, in his penetrating study *The Principles of History Teaching* (Methuen, 1963), warns us against adopting methods of teaching without looking at the philosophic and psychological assumptions behind them. In local history there is a great danger of becoming blinkered by parish affairs, of moving mountains to discover a pebble. A student recently wrote an outstanding dissertation based largely on primary sources: his subject was a village community in the 1890s, and the only issue that disturbed the somnolence of the village was the bitter dispute that raged in the Parish Council over the positioning of a stile. Similarly, children can spend a vast amount of time and ingenuity in creating or discovering something of little value – except of course to themselves.

Teachers are aware of this danger, but at the same time they know that the true value of an activity may not lie solely in the end-product. The use of a child's skills and imagination in creating a picture of village life or in composing a scrap-book on railways can be as important as the actual content of a study. Teachers must try to steer a middle course. W. E. Tate, one of the keenest practitioners of local history, advises us that 'the temptation to devote a year or more solely to the study of the school locality, alluring as it may be, is usually one to be resisted'. Local studies can be spaced out throughout a child's career in school and, taken in moderation, can very often provide an essential spur and inspiration when class teaching is flagging.

As local studies in schools have become more popular and indeed fashionable, there has been some attempt to assist teachers. More and more county record offices have established schools' advisers, and in the same way local museums have become more aware of the schools' needs and have responded to them. But for every twenty books and articles advising teachers that they *should* introduce local history into schools, there has been barely one showing them how to do it. One practical book which is extremely valuable is *Local History and the Teacher* by R. Douch (Routledge, 1967). In this book, Mr

[1] These dangers are lucidly argued by J. D. Marshall in *The Amateur Historian*, Vol. 6, No. 1, 1963.

Douch reviews the major sources of local history, and in the latter part he outlines comprehensive and ambitious schemes already attempted in colleges, secondary and junior schools.

Local history in the classroom

Clearly, the way in which local studies are used will depend on the range of the facilities available. A school in a large industrial town may have first-hand material on the Industrial Revolution, while a primary school teacher in a rural school may have the chance to explore a Roman villa or a castle. In a general sense, there are three ways in which local studies can be used in the classroom:

1. As vivid illustrations of a subject of national significance, such as the part played in the Civil War by local militias, canal development in the 18th century, or architectural changes in the last 200 years.
2. As a course in its own right, e.g., in the first year of a secondary school, in the sixth form (as part of a general studies course), or in the primary school. The advantage of a programme of this kind is that children of all ages can be introduced to sources of history – books and documents, archaeological remains and fieldwork.
3. As part of an integrated course such as environmental studies, in which history, geography and natural science are combined. This approach is becoming more popular in primary schools, largely because of the opportunity it offers for individual and original work.

Whatever the type of programme that a teacher arranges, the success achieved by pupils will be directly related to the amount of careful lesson preparation that teachers undertake beforehand. One must try to strike a balance between conscientious preparation by the teacher of oral lessons and of assignments which allow children to make discoveries for themselves; this balance is not easy to achieve.

It is unlikely that there will be a book suitable for class use. Most local histories are prolix and are written for adult readers. If a teacher wants a textbook he must write his own. Better still, he should be prepared to collect varied materials from various sources – books from the local library, photocopies of documents from the CRO, exhibits on loan from the museum, and above all, information accumulated by himself and his pupils over the years.

The planning will, of course, depend on the type of work the teacher intends to follow up. If he wants to illustrate the Civil War by referring to local battles, skirmishes and loyalties, he will have to search out the details in a general county history and look around museums and libraries for material. If on the other hand he wants his pupils to make a deeper study of the locality, he must be prepared to comb the County Record Office, explore the area himself and enlist the support of the library staff and perhaps of the Local Authority. Having made a preliminary survey, he has to collect the material, draw up work schemes and questionnaires, and map out his investigation. Many local studies break down because a pupil begins enthusiastically with a study of, for instance, Great Staughton in the Tudor period, and then finds that the evidence is scarce or indecipherable.

'Local' can be fairly widely interpreted. In terms of a definition, it might be said to cover an area which is within a pupil's experience either on foot or by coach. The county, town or parish come within this definition, but the 'north-east' or the 'south-west' may be equally suitable if the theme is a more general one, such as transport.

Practical difficulties will also arise during the course of the studies, and many teachers argue that these obstacles make local history a non-starter in schools. For instance, some LEAs and Headmasters make it difficult for children to be taken out of school during school hours. The Newsom Report recommended that visits should be encouraged and made a regular feature of secondary school teaching. If teachers begin in a small way, with a visit to a castle, canal or wool mill, and follow this up with substantial and impressive work in the classroom, Headmasters will probably become less suspicious of outside visits. Otherwise, if the LEA or the timetable defeat ingenuity, the children must be encouraged to make visits in their own time, at weekends or in the vacations. In my experience, once a pupil becomes enthusiastic about his project, he will be ready to follow it up in his own time. The real test of local history, for the majority of teachers, is – can it work in the classroom? There are thousands of different answers to this question, all in the affirmative, which have been discovered by individual teachers [1] Local history can be made both effective and practical. Here are some suggestions.

[1] One teacher's scheme is described by Gillian Preston in *The Value of Local History in the School Curriculum*, in *Teaching History*, Vol. 1, No. 2, November 1969.

Outside school: visits

1. Visits to places of historical importance. The value and organisation of outside visits are discussed elsewhere, but for any visit to be part of the training in observation, inquiry and reporting, children's activities have to be carefully prepared through work-cards, printed sheets of questions, information, and illustrations.
2. Visits to the Record Office to see an exhibition or to do some elementary work on source material.
3. Individual visits: by a school History Society or in the pupils' own time.

Inside school

1. Projects: local history lends itself to work by individuals or in groups – the history of the town, transport, streets, buildings, famous local men, industry, agriculture and communications.
2. Maps: by obtaining photocopies of old tithe and enclosure maps, town-plans or 19th century Ordnance Survey maps, children can be given practical work based on them.
3. Class exhibitions: taking a theme such as Victorian Leeds or Georgian Bath, children amass their own objects for display, write up scrapbooks, construct wall-friezes and draw pictures.

In junior schools

There is no reason why the study of the locality should not be linked to children's learning at an early age. However, the most satisfying work, as one might expect, can be accomplished with the older primary children. Here are some suggestions, based on local studies carried out in primary schools.

1. Class museum: children collect objects relevant to local history – postcards, pictures, cuttings from newspapers, handbills, books and curios. The child who brings the object should be encouraged to talk about it, and then each object can be part of the general scheme of work.
2. Information: the class teacher provides a basic broadsheet of information, with follow-up questions which children must answer by looking for information in books. Again, lists of questions based on books borrowed from the town or school library would serve the same purpose.
3. Visits to museums and historical sites: these can be linked to themes such as the Prehistoric and Roman settlements, the medieval town, the town in the 18th and 19th centuries, etc.
4. Classbook or scrapbook: groups or individuals add their contributions to a classbook. Some of the themes which might be covered are: famous men of the town; Victorian houses; local industries; the railway station; hospitals; almshouses; schools; local industries; the Town Hall; coaching inns; churches.
5. Models: models of the town or some of the buildings in it, or a portrayal of a period in the history of the town, the valley or the village can be constructed.

In secondary schools

In secondary schools the difficulties of reading are not so great, and teachers can be more ambitious, both in their choice of materials and in the complexity of children's work. In *Archives and Education*, HMSO, 1968, pp. 7-12, there are a number of reports from secondary school masters and mistresses of ambitious projects attempted and completed. Some of the ideas that have been tried and found to be successful might be summarised:

1. Scrapbooks: children are set topics similar to those listed for use in primary schools, but the subjects such as hospitals or roads would be treated more historically.
2. Buildings: subjects such as housing patterns in the towns – Georgian, Victorian, the suburbs of the 1930s, local authority housing – could all serve as topics for work or discussion. Individual buildings might be examined – churches, abbeys, castles, industrial sites, canals, railways – and brief histories written about them.
3. Group topics: titles such as 'Our Village in the Middle Ages', 'The Civil War in the County', 'Roman Cleethorpes', 'Life in Grandmother's Day' and so on offer the chance of individual work.[1]
4. The study of local documents – see chapter 5.
5. Imaginative reconstructions: eyewitness accounts of some past events in the history of the county or town, on the lines of a fictitious local newspaper for 1536, 1642, 1815 and 1918.
6. Sketches: children can make a pictorial record, in water colours, pen and ink, or other materials, of historical buildings in the locality and write about them.

Other schemes have included brass-rubbings, tape-recordings, and writing guide-books for imaginary visitors to places of local interest.

---

[1] Note a scheme described by T. D. Cook in *Local History: Some Practical Approaches*, in *Teaching History*, Vol. 1, No. 3.

Sources

Books

In their search for teaching material, most teachers would turn first to books. For the teacher there are the recommendations to be found in W. G. Hoskins, *Local History in England*, Longmans, 1959, and in J. West, *Village Records*, Macmillan, 1962. R. B. Pugh in *How to Write a Parish History*, 6th edition, Allen and Unwin, 1954, deals with a wide selection of written sources. The past numbers of *The Amateur Historian* (now *The Local Historian*), published quarterly by the National Council of Social Service, 26 Bedford Square, London, W.C.1, are extremely valuable. Similarly, the publications of the Historical Association: the *Local History Handlist* by F. W. Kuhlicke and F. G. Emmison (editors), 1965, and the *Short Guides to Records*, edited by L. Munby, are useful.

One's local library can usually make available a list of selected books on local affairs. As a guide to library sources, the teacher might consult J. L. Hobbs, *Local History and the Library*, Deutsch, 1962. In looking for printed material for class use the teacher has two objectives in mind: the books he can use, and the books that the children can use. There will be many books on the shelves of the local town library which will be useless from both viewpoints, and the teacher will only discover this by experience. There are short cuts, however, and the advice of the librarian is to be heeded.

The various county histories and the Victoria County History (published by the Institute of Historical Research, Senate House, London, W.C.1) are very largely reference books for the teacher, but secondary school pupils can use them as encyclopaedias, although some of the volumes are fifty years old and some of the latest ones still concentrate too heavily on the churches, the estates of the major landowners and family histories, rather than on social and economic changes. Nor, of course, is the Victoria County History complete. Despite these limitations, the VCH is a valuable quarrying ground.

Beyond this there are the stalwart county histories. In 1570 Christopher Saxton began working on the first national map to be published in Britain. Six years later, when it was published, William Lambarde completed the first great county history, *The Perambulation of Kent*. In the 200 years between 1576 and 1800 some fifty of these large, ponderous volumes were published. Among them were Carew's *Cornwall* (1602),

Dugdale's *Warwickshire* (1656), Thoroton's *Nottinghamshire* (1677), Aubrey's *Surrey* (1719) and Rudder's *Gloucestershire* (1779). Like the VCH, these tomes are valuable sources of information. The modern equivalents are lightweight, but are easier to read and have illustrations. The *Queen's* (or *King's*) *England* series (Hodder and Stoughton) and the *County Books* series (Robert Hale) come into this category. *The Making of the English Landscape* series (Hodder and Stoughton), edited by W. G. Hoskins, is extremely good for class use, but unfortunately only a handful of counties have been covered. The volume on *Gloucestershire* by H. P. R. Finberg is a brilliant analysis and could well provide the textbook that the teacher is looking for. Otherwise the *County Histories* by Darwen Finlayson have clear illustrations, maps and a text designed for class use, but again only six or so counties have been covered.

The various histories of the cities, towns and parishes have to be examined critically and on the spot. There is not a great deal of point in making any comment about them in general. Outside the general histories, the city or the county may be fortunate in having specialised studies – folklore, Roman antiquities, earthworks, enclosure, railway development, place-names and so on. Sources that should not be neglected are the scrapbooks or collections published by Women's Institutes and Community Councils. Scorned by academic historians but extremely useful in the classroom are three other series: the *Red Guides* (Ward Lock), the *Little Guides* (Methuen) and the *Shell Guides* (Faber). If these volumes can be purchased cheaply second-hand, they provide useful books for the school or class library. Otherwise, there are the *County Books* (Hale), the *County Guides* by Penguin and the *Face of Britain* and *Cities and Towns* books, published by Batsford.

Societies and periodicals

Teachers ought to be members of the local branch of the Historical Association (Head Office, 59a Kensington Park Road, London, S.E.11) and the local history or archaeological society which may be in existence in his area. Their *Papers* or *Transactions* will be useful sources of information on specialised topics. As an additional aid, the National Council of Social Service (26 Bedford Square, London, W.C.1) has published a series of pamphlets, of which *A Directory of Authorities and Organisations* and *Local History for Students* are useful numbers.

Newspapers

Newspapers can be an extremely useful source of material, and most municipal libraries have files of local newspapers, often going back as far as the mid-eighteenth century. Photocopies of pages from a newspaper are invaluable for town development, local politics, street-names, place-names, people, advertisements and the local slant on national events.

Archives

Most teachers will not remain content with books alone. Much of the colour and the human interest comes from manuscripts. However, both children and their teachers need to know the purposes for which these documents were written. This may fairly easily be achieved by referring to West's *Village Records*, Emmison's *Archives and Local History* (Methuen, 1966) and the *Amateur (Local) Historian*.

A full list of Record Offices is published in *Record Repositories in Great Britain* (HMSO, 1967). Most teachers will be well satisfied with the resources of their City or County Record Office but some records may be scattered in various record offices. The major ones are:

The Public Record Office, Chancery Lane, London, W.C.2

The British Museum, Great Russell Street, London, W.C.1

The House of Lords Record Office, House of Lords, London, S.W.1

The history teacher who wants to find source material suitable for use in schools would be well advised to turn first to the CRO. Almost all English counties and major cities now have a record office and some – Essex, Kent and Lancashire among others – have officers appointed specifically to assist schools.

The staff of the County Record Office can help in various ways. They will be able to advise on the choice of documents suitable for class use; they can decipher difficult words or phrases and suggest lines of research. An explanation of some of the services offered by CROs is contained in pp. 37-40 of this book. Otherwise, *County Records* by F. G. Emmison and I. Gray, published by the Historical Association, has a comprehensive guide.

Books suitable for school use

Allen A., *Story of the Village*, Faber, 1947

Bailey K. V., *Exploring the Past*, Studio Vista

Deverson H. J., and Lampitt R., *The Map that came to Life*, OUP 1967

Fletcher G. S., *Town's Eye View*, Hutchinson

Gordon H. A., *Key to Old Houses*, Murray, 1955

Grigson G., *Looking and Finding*, Phoenix

Harvey K., and Westell W. P., *Look and Find Out; Unwritten History and How to Read It*, Macmillan

Lindley K. A., *Town, Time and People*, Phoenix, 1962

Martin E. W., *The Book of the Village*, Phoenix

Martin E. W., *The Book of the Country Town*, Phoenix

Osmond E., *A Valley Grows Up*, OUP

Sauvain P. A., *Exploring at Home*, Hulton, 1966

Smallcombe W. A., *Archaeology for Young People*, Harrap, 1961

Tate W. E., *His Worship the Mayor*, OUP

Trent C., *Exploring the Countryside*, Phoenix, 1962

Vince J. N. T., *History All Around You*, Wheaton

References

The Amateur (Local) Historian, The National Council for Social Service, on behalf of the Standing Conference on Local History, 26 Bedford Square, London, W.C.1

Archives and Education, Education Pamphlet No. 54, Department of Education and Science, HMSO, 1968

Bonham Carter V., *Exploring Parish Churches*, Routledge, 1961

Celoria F., *Teach Yourself Local History*, EUP, 1958

Douch R., *Local History and the Teacher*, Routledge, 1967

Douch R., and Steer F. W., *Local History Essays: Notes for Students*, University of Southampton Institute of Education, 1960

Emmison F. G., *Archives and Local History*, Methuen, 1966

Emmison F. G., *How to Read Local Archives*, Historical Association, 1967

Emmison F. G., and Gray I. E., *County Records*, Historical Association, revised edition, 1968

Finberg J., *Exploring Villages*, Routledge, 1958

Gooder E. A., *Latin for Local History*, Longmans, 1961

Hobbs J. L., *Local History and the Library*, Deutsch, 1962

Hoskins W. G., *Local History in England*, Longmans, 1959

Humphreys D. W., and Emmison F. G., *Local History for Students*, NCSS, 1966

Kuhlicke F. W., and Emmison F. G., *English Local History Handlist*, Historical Association, 1965

Moorsom N., *Local History in a Town School*, Amateur Historian, Vol. 6, No. 7, 1965

Northeast P., *Local History in a Village School*, Amateur Historian, Vol. 6, No. 7, 1965

Pugh R. B., *How to Write a Parish History*, Allen and Unwin, 1954

Tate W. E., *The Parish Chest*, CUP, 1960

Wake J., *How to Compile a History . . . of Village Life*, 1935

West J., *Village Records*, Macmillan, 1962

Zoeftig S. H., *These Juniors go Exploring in History*, Forum, Vol. 2, 1960.

Children's work

It is not difficult to devise work schemes linked to documents illustrating aspects of local history. Three examples are given on these next pages:

An extract from a 19th century Directory;
A committal order;
A petition against the introduction of a police force.

Marshfield, Gloucestershire – Slater's Royal National and Commercial Directory, 1852-3

In this extract from a 19th century Directory for a small Gloucestershire village, Marshfield, one can see the many opportunities that there are for practical work by children on the sources of local history. The extract can be used to introduce the topic of the village in the 19th century through these questions, which could be attached to the photocopy.

1. Draw a map to show Marshfield in relation to London, Bath, Chippenham, Box and Bristol.
2. Compare the information in the Directory with the one-inch Ordnance Survey map today. What differences do you notice?
3. What were the major occupations in the village when this Directory was written?
4. What different religious organisations are represented in the village?
5. Compare this document with the Electoral Roll for today which can be consulted in the Library. How many of the surnames shown in the list of residents are represented in the village today?
6. Draw or paint a picture of the main street of the village, showing an inn, a school, a church or chapel, the post office, and a selection of the shops. Name each building, selecting the name from the information contained in the document.

The village school in Marshfield could of course do some fieldwork based on this extract. They could discover how many of the chapels, schools, inns and shops were still to be found in the village; or they could look up the names on the tombstones in the churchyard or in the registers and draw up a modern edition of Slater's Directory.

Committal order

Children can be asked to read the document and to answer questions about it. Alternatively, the order could be linked to a picture of a prison in the early 19th century or an account of an escape from prison, and pupils could be asked to make comments about it.

Questions that might be asked on this committal order are:

1. What crime was Edward Mott convicted of by the justices?
2. What is the name today for 'a house of correction'?
3. Do you think Edward Mott's punishment was harsh or fair? Say why you think so.
4. What would a prisoner have to do for 'hard labour'?
5. What reasons can you give for a person such as Edward Mott being driven to crime in 1826?
6. Draw or paint pictures of two scenes:
   (a) the inside of a prison in 1826;
   (b) the court scene, as Edward Mott was sentenced.

At first sight this committal order appears to have very little value for the classroom. However, a few simple questions added to it involve the pupil immediately in analysing an original document, allowing him to make judgements based on evidence and to express his ideas and opinions in his own way. The order can thus be used to introduce children to law and order in early 19th century England, the reasons for the lawlessness, the attitude of the courts, prison life and perhaps the origin of the police force.

Petition against the introduction of the Police Force

Having used the committal order, the teacher can then carry over the opinions and information to another local issue of importance – the introduction of the police force.

In this document, the landowners of a small Gloucestershire village, Ampney Crucis, vigorously oppose the creation of a local force. The

MARSHFIELD

IS a parish, and the only one, in the upper division of Thornbury hundred—the market town, a small one, is 103 miles w. by s. from London, on the road to Bristol, from which it is distant 12 miles: by this road, the distance between these two cities is shorter by five miles than through Bath, which lies about seven miles to the south. It is situated at one of the south-east angles of Gloucestershire, where Wilts and Somerset meet the first-named county; and about 4½ miles N.W. from Box station, on the Great Western railway. The town consists of one street, about half a mile in length. Malting is the chief trade of the place, and the produce of the land in its vicinity is almost confined to barley.

The parish church of Saint Mary is an ancient and handsome structure, in the later style of English architecture, with a fine square tower at the western end: the living is a discharged vicarage, in the gift of the Warden and Fellows of New College Oxford; the Rev. George Sherer is the present incumbent. There are a chapel each for Independents, Unitarians, and Primitive Methodists; two or three public schools (one of which is endowed), and almshouses for eight aged and indigent men and women. The market is now but little attended. Fairs, May 24th, for horned cattle, and October 24th, for horses, sheep and cheese. The parish contained in 1831, 1,631 inhabitants, and in 1814, 1,674.

POST OFFICE, Joseph Davis, *Post Master.*—Letters from all parts arrive (from CHIPPENHAM) every morning at nine, and are despatched thereto at half-past four in the afternoon.

GENTRY AND CLERGY.
Cordington Sir William, Bart., Donnington
Holbarrow Isaac, Esq. Marshfield
Horlick William, Esq. Ashwick
Hume Robert, Esq. (magistrate), Marshfield
Mallock Rev. Rawlin, Marshfield
Toghill Mr. George, Marshfield
Wrangham Serjeant Digby, Esq., Rocks

ACADEMIES AND SCHOOLS.
Bryans Mary & Sarah (boarding)
FREE SCHOOL, Thomas Canvin, master
Gibbons John (boarding and day)
INDEPENDENT SCHOOL, Tabitha Ellson, mistress
INFANTS' SCHOOL (church), Elizabeth Rawlins and Esther Gale, teachers
Taylor Olive (day)

PROFESSIONAL PERSONS.
Bridges William R. surgeon
Huff Robert A., registrar of births and deaths
Smith John, attorney
Wilkins William, surgeon

INNS AND PUBLIC HOUSES.
Angel, William Cainbourne
Catherine Wheel Inn, Samuel Adams
Coddrington Arms Inn, (and inland revenue office), Joseph Davis
Crown, George Russell
George, Joshua Burcombe
Lord Nelson, George England
Star, Benjamin Bedford
White Hart, Betty Beaman

MALTSTERS.
Allen Henry
Bedford Worthy
Camery Thomas
Downes William
Elms Edward
Wait Daniel
Woodward and Golding (and brewers)

SHOPKEEPERS & TRADERS.
Allen Henry, grocer
Allpass William, boot & shoemaker
Balch James, butcher
Bane William, saddler
Barton Jane, earthenware dealers
Benjamin Robert, shopkeeper
Bodman Charles, draper and grocer
Bond James, draper, and agent to the British Empire Assurance Office
Bond Mary, milliner
Broomfield Eliza, dressmaker
Burcombe James, stone mason
Burcombe Joshua, butcher
Burcombe Peter, stone mason
Davies Thomas, blacksmith
Davis William, tailor
Fry John, baker
Furney William, revenue officer
Hamilton William, tailor
Hancock John, boot and shoemaker
Hancock William, shoe maker and shopkeeper
Hathrell Isaac, basket maker
Hulbert Benjamin, watchmaker
Jefferies Thomas, shopkeeper
Jefferies William, carpenter
Jenkins Esther, draper and grocer
Jones James B. boot & shoe maker
Jones John, shoe maker
Jones William, police sergeant
Oskwell William, hatter
Parker John & Robert, plumbers and glaziers
Parker Robert C. draper and grocer
Poole Thomas, hair dresser
Salmon John, boot and shoemaker
Sidnel Caroline, grocer
Smith William, stone mason
Sweatman Thos. Comley, shopkeeper
Sweatman William, baker and confectioner
Taylor John, painter and glazier
Thompson John, saddler
White Thomas, butcher
Willshire Amelia, shopkeeper
Wimbow Stephen, tailor
Woodland John, chemist & stationer
Woodward & Golding, brewers

CONVEYANCE BY RAILWAY, ON THE GREAT WESTERN LINE. *Station,* at Box, about 4½ miles s.e. from Marshfield.

CARRIER.
To BATH, Nathaniel Banes, Wednesday and Saturday, and to BRISTOL, on Thursday.

A nineteenth century directory
By courtesy of the British Museum

COUNTY OF
Gloucester
TO the Constable of *Cheltenham* in the said County, and to the Keeper of the House of Correction at *Northleach* in the said County.

FORASMUCH as *Edward Mott* late of

is duly convicted before *us two* of the Justices of our Lord the King, assigned to keep the Peace, within the said County of Gloucester. *on the Oath of Martha Large as a Rogue and Vagabond for that he the said Edward Mott was on Saturday night last found in the dwelling house of William Taylor in Cheltenham aforesaid with intent to commit a Felony therein and upon his examination not giving a good account of himself*

said *Edward Mott* These are therefore to command you to carry the to the said House of Correction at *Northleach* and deliver h... to the said Keeper thereof, together with this Warrant. And *we* do hereby command you the said Keeper to receive the said *Edward Mott* into your Custody in the said House of Correction and him there safely to keep *to hard labour for the space of three Months from the date hereof*

Given under *our* hands and seal At *Cheltenham* in the said County of Gloucester, the *30* day of *August* in the *7th* year of the Reign of our Sovereign Lord King *George the fourth* and in the year of our Lord One Thousand, Eight Hundred and *twenty six*

Wm Hicks — *Wm Hobbes*

The committal of Edward Mott
By courtesy of Gloucestershire County Council

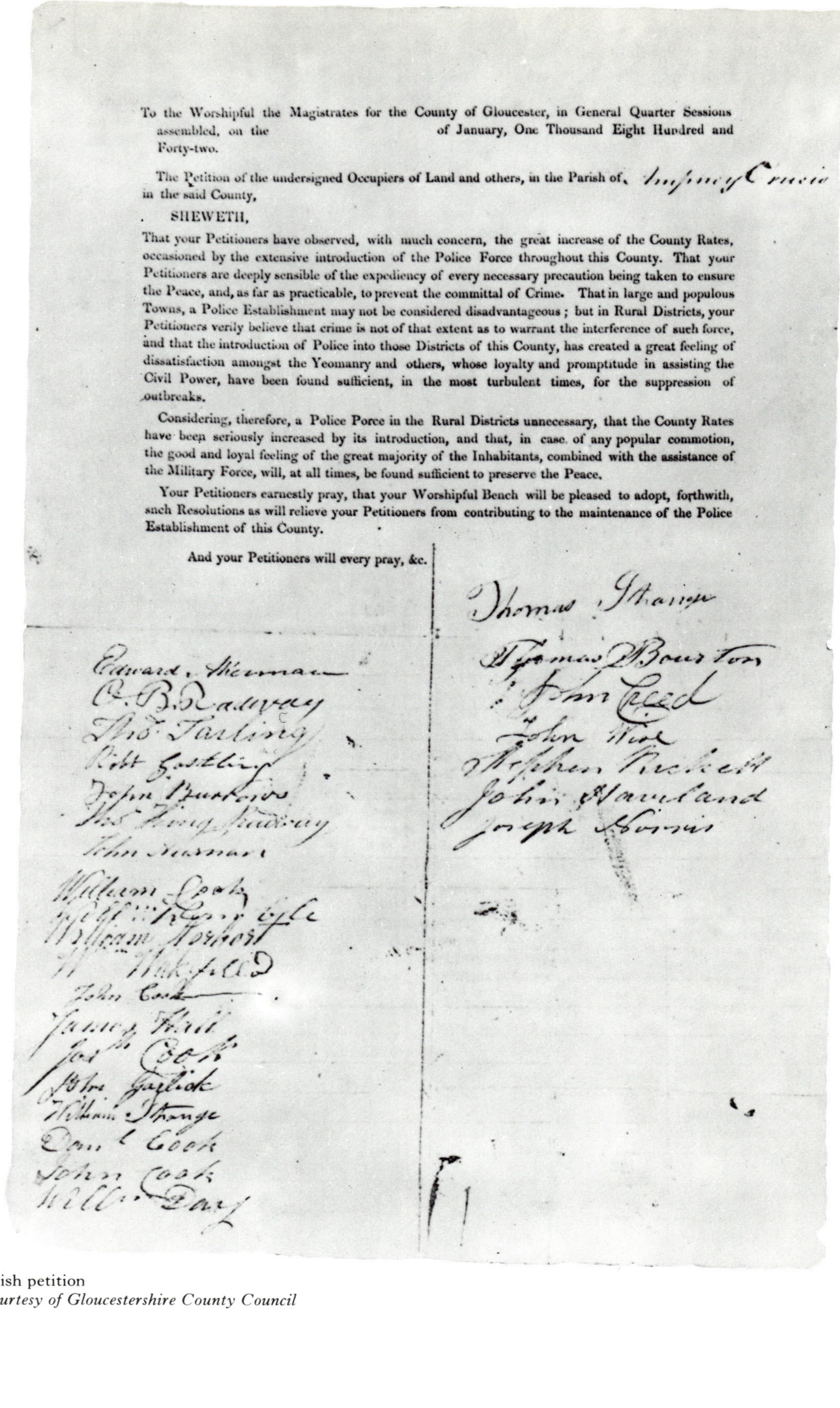

To the Worshipful the Magistrates for the County of Gloucester, in General Quarter Sessions assembled, on the _____ of January, One Thousand Eight Hundred and Forty-two.

The Petition of the undersigned Occupiers of Land and others, in the Parish of *Ampney Crucis* in the said County,

 SHEWETH,

That your Petitioners have observed, with much concern, the great increase of the County Rates, occasioned by the extensive introduction of the Police Force throughout this County. That your Petitioners are deeply sensible of the expediency of every necessary precaution being taken to ensure the Peace, and, as far as practicable, to prevent the committal of Crime. That in large and populous Towns, a Police Establishment may not be considered disadvantageous; but in Rural Districts, your Petitioners verily believe that crime is not of that extent as to warrant the interference of such force, and that the introduction of Police into those Districts of this County, has created a great feeling of dissatisfaction amongst the Yeomanry and others, whose loyalty and promptitude in assisting the Civil Power, have been found sufficient, in the most turbulent times, for the suppression of outbreaks.

Considering, therefore, a Police Force in the Rural Districts unnecessary, that the County Rates have been seriously increased by its introduction, and that, in case of any popular commotion, the good and loyal feeling of the great majority of the Inhabitants, combined with the assistance of the Military Force, will, at all times, be found sufficient to preserve the Peace.

Your Petitioners earnestly pray, that your Worshipful Bench will be pleased to adopt, forthwith, such Resolutions as will relieve your Petitioners from contributing to the maintenance of the Police Establishment of this County.

 And your Petitioners will every pray, &c.

[Column of signatures, left:]
Edward Akerman
C. B. Ramvay
Ths Tarling
Robt Gastling
John Hawkins
Ths Long Sudbury
John Akerman

William Cook
Will Henry Cole
William Norbert
W Wakefield
John Cook
James Trail
Josh Cook
John Garlick
William Strange
Danl Cook
John Cook
Will Dancy

[Column of signatures, right:]
Thomas Strange
Thomas Bourton
John Ceed
John Nve
Stephen Prickett
John Haviland
Joseph Norris

A parish petition
By courtesy of Gloucestershire County Council

petition could well be used in conjunction with a class lesson on Sir Robert Peel and the formation of police forces in England and Wales, or merely as a pointer to some aspects of village life in the mid-19th century.

Questions that might be asked, either as a questionnaire pinned to the photocopy of the document or orally in class, might be:

1. What are the objections of the petitioners to the introduction of a police force in the village?

2. Why should the Yeomanry be dissatisfied?

3. For what other purposes, apart from the police, would the county rate be used in 1842? What additional items fall on the rates today?

4. What is the connection between the police in Ampney Crucis and Sir Robert Peel?

5. In the signatures, one family name occurs five times and another two names occur twice. Which are they? What are the most popular Christian names?

Chapter Four

The Use of Sources

The use of source material in the teaching of history has been long advocated and long practised. In the past, however, documents have been largely restricted to sixth forms and university courses. It has been felt that children under the age of sixteen could not read original documents or even understand those in printed form. This opinion has been effectively refuted in recent years by the work that younger children have been able to accomplish with manuscript records; what once depended on the enthusiasm and initiative of the individual teacher has now become part of the school textbook empire. In the flood of printed books, collections of documents and folders of source material, the teacher might well lose himself, and it is pertinent to consider the objectives and uses of source material in the light of recent research and publications.[1]

The aims of such methods are to provide children with the original material from which history is constructed – letters, newspapers, contemporary accounts, maps, Acts of Parliament, Reports, portraits, engravings and cartoons – in the hope that the imagination and interest of children will be aroused by contact with the exciting raw material of history. In this way, documents (or rather, photocopies, Xerox copies or photographs of documents) can serve as fascinating and lively illustrations. In *Archives and Education* (HMSO, 1968) the authors write that, 'the original letter or document is charged with an emotion, an urgency and an immediacy, to which the later printed record can never pretend. For a child to read of the torture of Guido Fawkes is one thing; it is another to see the firm signature to his examination of Novem-

ber 8th and the faltering half-completed effort of November 10th, written after the execution of the king's warrant, to use "the gentler torture first, *et sic per gradus ad ima tenditur*". That Nelson really did lose an arm at Santa Cruz becomes emphatically clear when we see his right- and left-handed letters. At least for some – and probably for more than is generally imagined – the original document, letter or journal is the best door into the past.'

However, there is another equally laudable intention behind the use of records. A skilful teacher can use documents and pictures as materials for intellectual exercises. It is not beyond the wit and ability of children, both in secondary schools and in the upper forms of primary schools, to use documents to analyse, assess and evaluate. Some examples of this technique are given in this book.

Of course, one dare not claim too much from this method of teaching. Schoolboys and schoolgirls are not historians. There is little point in introducing pupils to documents that they cannot read. Like any other method of teaching, the use of source material requires careful preparation by the teacher. Most records are written in a strange language. Latin or Old English was the language of documents written before 1066, Latin or Norman-French after the Conquest. Styles of handwriting pose great problems. Various forms of 'court hand' were used from the 13th century onwards, and from 1500 to about 1700 the secretary hand, widely used in formal documents, is very difficult to decipher. However, from about 1740 handwriting is really not much more difficult to read than a modern hand, although legal terms and formal phrasing may pose problems. Therefore the teacher can use documents dating from the mid-eighteenth

[1] E. R. Lloyd in *The Amateur Historian*, Vol. 7, No. 2, 1966: *The Use of Historical Documents in Schools*.

century. By 'documents' one means photocopies – by Xerox, microfilm or photographic prints – of original material. These copies can be obtained from most county record offices and from the major national repositories such as the PRO, the British Museum and the House of Lords Record Office. There are, of course, printed editions of documents and although these have value in the classroom, copies of originals lend far more immediacy and stimulation.

A third objective in using documentary material is to introduce more variety into history teaching and to release children from the stereotyped textbook. Children are more likely to respond to methods of learning which involve the exercise of the imagination and which give them opportunities for practical work.

Printed sources

Where does one begin? A large amount of varied documentary evidence is readily available in print. The two major guides to this material are: R. Somerville, *Handlist of Record Publications* (British Records Association, 1951) and E. L. C. Mullins, *Texts and Calendars* (Royal Historical Society, 1958). The latter book lists publications under the various societies that produce them: the Navy Records Society, for instance, publishes volumes of naval documents.

In assessing the quality of printed source material, the teacher must be sure of his objectives. Lively accounts, relevance to the topic being discussed, opportunity for practical work based on the documents – these are the criteria on which one might base selection. There are very many collections of documents in print and one cannot list them all here, especially as many concern themselves with a special theme – G. R. Elton's *The Tudor Constitution* (CUP, 1960), or R. H. Tawney and E. Power's *Tudor Economic Documents* (ULP, 1951), for instance. Some schools and libraries might still have the volumes by M. W. Keatinge, who was one of the pioneers in the use of source material. In *A History of England for Schools with Documents, Problems and Exercises* (Black, 1911), Keatinge (in conjunction with N. L. Frazer and D. G. Perry) tried the experiment of linking extracts with class work, but his idea lapsed and most recent writers and publishers have been content to make a collection of documents and leave their use in the classroom to the teacher's imagination and initiative.

For the use of teachers and sixth formers, the twelve volumes of *English Historical Documents* published by Eyre and Spottiswoode under the editorship of Professor D. C. Douglas will be invaluable for the upper levels of secondary schools. However, for classroom use further down the school, the *Anvil* series of source books, published (in paperback) by Van Nostrand in the USA, gives a brief history followed by a group of selected documents. One of the titles in this series is *Fifty Major Documents of the 20th Century*. Booklets that are to be used as supplements to the textbook or as a basis for an introduction to sources are contained in the *Archives Series* (Arnold). Extracts from newspapers, letters, diaries, speeches, novels, Acts of Parliament and treaties are given: titles published in this series include *Hitler and the Rise of the Nazis* and *Disraeli and Conservatism*. Rather older, but again valuable collections of documents are contained in Robinson and Beard's *Readings in Modern European History* (Ginn). J. S. Millward's *Portraits and Documents* (Hutchinson) and R. Breach's *Documents and Descriptions* (OUP) are more recent publications. Royston Pike is editing documents of the 18th and 19th centuries: *Human Documents of the Industrial Revolution* is one in the series and provides an illuminating picture of the horrors of working class life in England during the Industrial Revolution. Two other valuable collections are contained in the *History Alive Source Books* published by Blond, and *Society and Industry in the nineteenth century* by the Oxford University Press.

Collections of documents on special subjects are legion. Now sadly out of print is J. Dover Wilson's *Life in Shakespeare's England* first published by CUP in 1911 and later by Penguin. The *They Saw it Happen* series by Blackwell brings documents in readable form to the lower forms of secondary schools and *Problems in European Civilisation* (Harrap) presents documents chosen to illustrate opposing views of important and debatable subjects.

By far the most popular and successful method of bringing documents into the classroom has been the *Jackdaw* series published by Jonathan Cape. The pioneer in this field was John Langdon-Davies, who hit on the happy idea of arranging a folder of material – documents, some descriptive broadsheets, maps and diagrams – around a theme. The subjects have been varied: *The Battle of Trafalgar*, *Richard III*, *Young Shakespeare*, *The Plague and the Fire*, and so on. A large number of *Jackdaws* are now in print, and there are more on the way. What is their attraction? Do they serve only as a change from the normal routine? Are they useful only as illustrations?

In the first place, *Jackdaws* serve as brilliant classroom illustrations, which catch the attention and interest of children and create learning situations. Whether or not these opportunities are utilised depends on the initiative of the teacher, for the *Jackdaws* themselves give few clues to their possible uses. What these publications need are clearly designed work-cards or projects which direct children to specific tasks – reading sections in recommended books, answering questions on the documents, drawing, painting, following up clues, making their own Jackdaws, drafting their own Magna Carta or making judgements based on the evidence contained in the material. The *Jackdaws* make learning too easy, by providing the answers in the information sheets: they miss the opportunity to exploit the deep interest which they arouse. To be fair, there are questions set in a section headed 'Think for Yourself'. In many of the folders these questions are linked to the material. But the questions are not always suitable, nor are they always clear. For instance, the *Jackdaw* on *Hadrian's Wall* contains only eight documents and five broadsheets – not enough material for individual work in a class of thirty children. Although the five questions involve the use of the documents, imagination and some research, they do not provide a class with practical things to do. There are no suggestions for model-making, drawing, or painting, and there are no questions which require the children to analyse, assess or consider evidence.

To take another example, the two *Jackdaws* on the *French Revolution* (nine documents and seven broadsheets in each) seem to be directed at the sixth form, for some of the documents are in French (with translations and transcripts), and the questions are difficult: 'The Terror was the logical outcome of the successive breakdowns of revolutionary government. Do you agree?', and 'What general lesson about all revolutions can be drawn from the Terror?'.

On the other hand, *The Early Trade Unions* contains a fascinating collection of material and the questions are designed for a younger audience and invite original work. For instance:

1. See how many trade public houses there are in your area, for example, 'The Bricklayers' Arms' or 'Stonemasons' Rest'.

2. Make a list of the unions on whose members you depend, from the time you get up in the morning until the time you get to school.

This confusion of aim in the *Jackdaw* series prevents teachers from exploiting the full possibilities of a brilliant idea. At the same time one must say that *Jackdaws* have made a vital impact on history teaching and fully merit their success. One would like to see teachers devising their own Jackdaws. This can be done by collecting pictures from galleries or cutting them from the pages of *Pictorial Education*, adding photocopies of documents obtained from local record offices, museums or the Public Record Office, and linking the whole thing together with broadsheets, questionnaires and work-schemes which involve the children in practical activities. To illustrate the use of extracts, documents, pictures and other records, two examples of this sort of work are included. The first deals with the history of the Navy, and the second shows how an extract from an old newspaper or magazine can be an inspiration for children's work.

Nelson's Navy

These documents and illustrations reveal a darker side of naval life in Nelson's day. They can be used as part of a scheme of work on the Navy or as background material to a study of conditions at sea, leading up to Nelson and Trafalgar.

The first three documents deal with the problem of recruitment and the other two with punishment.

Recruitment was very difficult in the late eighteenth century: conditions in the fleet were so dangerous and barbaric that volunteers were rare and men had to be taken by force. The first extract is taken from *The Adventures of John Wetherell*, a seaman who was press-ganged into the navy in 1803 and who wrote a vivid journal of his grim life at sea.

'April 1, 1803. In this manner they obtained their ships' crews. On the first of April early in the morning our orders were to have our boats ready to go on shore after breakfast, in harbour boats' crews; accordingly three boats from our ship, three from the *Athelion* and four from the *Antelope* all started for the shore, having orders to fetch every man on board that was able to serve his King and country. They laid under the land until evening and then in great pomp made plunder as I term it. The market house was to be their prison, where a lieutenant was stationed

The liberty of the subject (Gillray)
By courtesy of the National Maritime Museum

THREE MEN FOR THE
NAVY.
WANTED

For the Townships of Chipping, Dutton,

And Clayton-le-Dale,

THREE ABLE-BODIED

Seamen or Landmen,

TO serve in his Majesty's NAVY during the present War only; and as the Time for accepting such Volunteers expires on *Wednesday* next, the 14th of *December*, it is hoped that no True-Born BRITISH TAR will lose so favourable an Opportunity. Such as make an immediate Application will be preferred, and over and above a handsome Bounty, will be entitled to, and receive, Advantages superior to any other Service, viz. The Families and Friends of Volunteers will receive Monthly Pay, and the Volunteers themselves will have a bountiful Supply of CLOATHING, BEEF, GROG, FLIP, and STRONG BEER, also a Certainty of PRIZE-MONEY, as the Men entered for this Service will be sent to Capture

The Rich Spanish Galleons,

and in Consequence will return loaded with DOLLARS and HONOURS, to spend their Days in PEACE and PLENTY.

H U Z Z A !!!

☞ BOUNTY will be paid by applying to JOHN SWINGLEHURST, of *Chipping*; THOMAS DEWHURST, of *Dutton*; and JAMES HIGGS, of *Clayton-le-Dale*.

BLACKBURN: J. WATERWORTH, PRINTER.

A recruitment poster
By courtesy of the National Maritime Museum

with a guard of marines and before daylight next morning their prison was full of all denominations, from the parish priest to the farmer in his frock and wooden shoes. Even the poor blacksmith, cobbler, tailor, barber, baker, fisherman and doctor were all dragged from their homes that night and without the least timely notice as on former meetings. All assembled in private to hold a nightly meeting in the market house. The assembly started round in terror and confusion at the sight of their President and Lieutenant and his attendants, the marines.

"What means all this fun?" says one.

"Holy Father!" cries the parson.

"We are all enchanted!" says the blacksmith.

"Why, the devil never wears arms!" says the cobbler.

"I think", says the barber, "there has been some invading enemy landed on the coast and intends to drag us all from our families and our homes and use us as slaves".'

In the picture *The Liberty of the Subject* the press-gang, led by the bosun's mate in the centre, have seized a number of landsmen (including a tailor, whose scissors can be seen peeping from his pocket) and are carrying them off to a ship.

The recruiting poster can be used in association with the other illustrations to show how voyages and ships were described in glowing terms in order to attract men to serve.

Children's work

1. Another recruiting poster, similar to the one shown here, described Jamaica, an island in the West Indies, as 'that delightful island, abounding in rum, sugar and Spanish dollars, where there is delicious living and plenty of grog and punch'. Design a recruiting poster offering inducements to men to volunteer for a voyage to the Mediterranean to raid Spanish and French shipping. What are 'British Tars', 'Grog', 'Punch', 'Flip' and 'Prize-money'?

2. How did the press-gang operate? Why was it hated? Why did men refuse to serve in the Navy of Nelson's day?

3. In the picture *The Liberty of the Subject* the tailor's wife is shown trying to save her husband from being carried off by the press-gang. Write a short story, with illustrations, about the tailor's adventures at sea, imagining that he sailed in the *Victory* and took part in the Battle of Trafalgar.

Punishment

An account of a flogging from *The Adventures of John Wetherell*, edited by C. S. Forester.

'John Markins another patient had to pass through the mill. Not pleasing Dennis Obriant, the Master's Mate while at work washing decks, Dennis calls old Cole the boatswain's mate, ordered him to take Markins forward and give him a good starting.[1] At this time Mrs. Markins was on board with her husband, and before Cole commenced his exercise poor Jack set up a horrid roar. This in one moment brought Sally on deck, and seeing her husband taking those nauseous bitters, knowing by his grinning and dancing they were not pleasant, Sally flies to the cabin door, crying out "Captain, they are killing my husband". The sentinel drove her away but not until she had roused the great Mogul who sent for the Officer of the Deck, learnt the whole, and gave orders to put Markins in irons. This done at seven bells "all hands to witness punishment". Markins was brought forth, ordered to strip down his pantaloons, and then they lashed him to a gun. Made Sally stand by his side until he had six dozen lashes on his bare posteriors. Great.'

The illustration by George Cruikshank shows a man being flogged, tied to a grating, with the whole ship's company drawn up on deck. The marines are to the left and the bosun and his mates, together with the ship's doctor, are standing behind the grating. The picture illustrates a story called 'The Point of Honour'. The wrong man has been accused of a crime on board ship, but just as he is about to be flogged, the true culprit has stepped forward and is tearing off his shirt in readiness for his punishment.

A scheme of work for children, based on these two documents, might be arranged as follows:

1. In John Wetherell's account of a flogging on board ship he uses some very odd expressions. What do these mean: 'sentinel', 'nauseous bitters', 'the great Mogul', and 'pantaloons'?

2. Imagine that you are a boy who has been press-ganged on board HMS *Hussar* (Wetherell's ship). Write a letter home, describing to your mother the hardships of life on board. Find out

[1] 'Starting' was a form of corporal punishment, used by the bosun and his mates to encourage men to start work. A blow with a rope's end was usually sufficient, but some petty officers carried a 'starter' – a two-foot length of line with a knot at the end.

The Point of Honor.

Ge! Cruikshank fes!

London — Pub!! July 1!! 1825 by J!! Robins & Co Ivy Lane — Pater noster Row —

from 'The Point of Honour' (George Cruikshank)
By courtesy of the National Maritime Museum

about food, clothing, health, accommodation and your work as a sailor from books on the navy.

3. Write down a list of reasons why it was considered necessary to have such strict discipline in the navy.

4. Write a short story about the incident shown in the picture 'A Point of Honour'. Illustrate the story with a painting or drawing.

The Illustrated London News, April 25 1857

These edited extracts from a magazine provide an opportunity to illustrate the use of contemporary newspapers. The major article on page 36 is on fashion. Questions can be quite easily devised to make children read and interpret the article and to add their own comments and descriptions. For instance:

1. If you like the clothes described here, explain why you do so. What would have been the disadvantages of wearing these clothes?

2. Draw a picture of some Victorian ladies strolling in the park, showing off their 'May fashions'. Make your drawing as accurate as possible, colouring the clothes according to the information given in the article.

3. Devise an advertisement, along the lines of those shown here, for 'Messrs. Jay and Smith, 246 Regent Street, London, Dressmaker and Hatter'.

The other items of information can also be linked to questions:

4. The Russian mortar, recently placed at Dover, was captured from the Russians. Which war does this refer to?

5. At Court, Queen Victoria is convalescing after the birth of a baby daughter. Who was the 'Prince Consort'? What was the tragedy connected with the Prince Consort some four years later that plunged the Queen and the Nation into deep gloom?

6. Draft two advertisements:
   (a) For a chemist, advocating the advantages of using Cod Liver Oil;
   (b) For the Theatre Royal, Shoreditch, London, advertising the visit by a company of actors performing plays by Shakespeare.

7. Later, in July 1857, there were a number of rebellions and mutinies by Indian troops and princes. Write a short article for the magazine, as if written by an eye-witness, and with illustrations, describing one or two events that took place in the Indian Mutiny.

THE COURT.

Her Majesty's recovery, we rejoice to announce, is complete. The bulletin issued on Monday was to the following gratifying effect:—

Buckingham Palace, April 20, 1857, 9 a.m.

The Queen is convalescent.
The infant Princess is well.

JAMES CLARK, M.D.
CHARLES LOCOCK, M.D.
ROBERT FERGUSON, M.D.

Her Majesty's recovery is so far advanced that no further bulletins will be issued. The members of the Royal family, the diplomatic corps, and the aristocracy continued to make inquiries until after this announcement was made public, since which, no further cause for anxiety existing, the calls at the Palace have become less frequent.

The Prince Consort and the younger members of the Royal family have taken daily riding and walking exercise. The Prince has made frequent visits to Gloucester House, to inquire after the health of his illustrious relative, the Duchess of Gloucester, generally accompanied by some of the youthful members of the Royal family.

On Wednesday the Queen had sufficiently recovered to receive visits from the Duchess of Kent and Princesses of Hohenlohe-Langenburg, when the latter took leave of her Majesty on their departure for the Continent.

The Marchioness of Ely has succeeded the Duchess of Wellington as the Lady in Waiting to her Majesty. The Hon. Mortimer Sackville West has relieved Colonel the Hon. A. N. Hood in his duties as the Groom in Waiting to the Queen.

FASHIONS FOR MAY.

THE new Spring Fashions have determined beyond a doubt that green and lilac are to be the prevailing colours of the season for out-door costume. These two hues are introduced either separately, or in combination, in dresses, bonnets, ribbons ; in short, in almost every article of costume. Several bonnets have been made of tulle *bouillonné*, with narrow bias folds of green or lilac silk. Between each *bouillonné* there is a double fold of silk, of graduated shades of colour. Green and lilac are the hues most effective for trimming bonnets of the style just mentioned. They should be ornamented at each side by a bouquet of flowers, or a feather of hues corresponding with those employed for the trimming. *Bouton d'or* and mallow colour are also very fashionable hues for trimming bonnets.

An extremely elegant bonnet has been made of terry velvet, of a very light shade of lilac, or, more properly, of peach-blossom. The front, which is rather open, is edged with a fall of white blonde turned back ; and in the inside of the front there is a narrow row of black blonde, falling downward. On each side of the crown there is a small bouquet of white marabouts, tipped with lilac. The inside trimming consists of a ruche of white blonde, with bouquets of shaded violets and strips of marabout.

Another much-admired bonnet is of white silk, edged round the front with shaded folds of green crape. At the lower part of the crown there is a broader fold of shaded green crape, edged at each side by a ruche of white tulle. At one side of the bonnet there is a cazoar head, terminated by a plume of white feathers tipped with variegated hues. The under trimming consists of bouquets of hawthorn, and a very full ruche of white tulle. The strings are of broad white sarcenet ribbon, edged with green.

Velvet cloaks of small size are at present very generally worn, and they form an appropriate intermediary wrap between the warm winter cloak and the summer mantelet. Large cashmere shawls are, as usual, much in favour at the present season. Many novel and elegant designs in cashmere shawls have lately appeared. The small velvet cloaks are mostly of the circular form. Some are edged with one or two rows of black lace, and others with very broad silk fringe.

The principal change in the make of dresses is perceptible in the sleeves. The pagodas, which have been for some time past superseded by other forms, are now beginning to recover fashion-

able favour. Pagodas, puffs, and the Greek style, may now be said to be all equally fashionable.

It has been mentioned that basques are not likely to be so generally worn as they have heretofore been. But this is a mistake. Scarcely any dresses, except those intended exclusively for ball or evening costume, are made without basques. They are of various shapes, and they present great diversity in the materials employed for trimming. Some are long, others short ; some are cut out in scallops, and are castellated at the edge. Fringe is a very favourite trimming, so also is passementerie, of which a new kind has been introduced for the purpose, consisting of round tufts of silk. The effect of this new trimming is at once novel and pretty. When lace is employed for trimming a basque it may either be set on nearly plain or very full. Narrow frills or ruches of silk form an appropriate trimming for the basque, when it corresponds with the style of trimming on the skirt of the dress.

The most fashionable riding-habits are of black or dark blue cloth. The newest style of corsage for riding-habits is without a basque, and the sleeves are made very wide at the ends. The collar and turned-up cuffs should be of fine lawn or cambric, finished with broad hems and a double row of hem-stitch. The hat should be of black felt, slightly turned up at each side, with a black plume waving towards the back of the head. A small *cravache* with an amber handle completes the costume.

Three of the objects represented in our Illustrations of Fashion — viz., the cloak (with patent spring hood), the fan parasol, and the bonnet — are engraved from drawings made by permission of Messrs. Jay and Smith, from articles in the elegant show-rooms of their Sponsalia, 246, Regent-street. The cloak which is shown on the first figure, on the right-hand side, is very elegant and becoming in form, but its peculiar recommendation is the perfect protection it affords to the head, without the risk of injuring, or even in the slightest degree disordering, the head-dress. Every lady must have experienced the discomfort, to say nothing of the danger, attendant on the sudden transition from a warm to a cold atmosphere, on leaving the Opera, an evening party, or any crowded assembly. The old-fashioned caleches, and the hoods of various kinds more recently introduced, have all been more or less liable to the objection of pressing upon, and consequently injuring, the flowers and other light ornaments composing the head-dress. The objection in question is completely obviated in the hood introduced by Messrs. Jay and Smith. It expands by means of elastic wires, thereby affording complete protection to the head, without close contact, or pressure on the *coiffure*. The touch of an invisible and ingeniously-contrived spring instantaneously

RUSSIAN MORTAR, RECENTLY PLACED AT DOVER.—(SEE NEXT PAGE)

from 'The Illustrated London News' April 25th, 1857
By courtesy of the Illustrated London News and Sketch Ltd.

36

Archives

If a teacher wants to collect his own material, where does he apply? For copies of documents, he must be prepared to look out his material in the Public Record Office, Chancery Lane, London, W.C.2, the British Museum, Great Russell Street, London, W.C.1, The House of Lords Record Office, Westminster, London, S.W.1, and the county record offices. Most of these offices can provide photographic copies of documents by a quick copying process, and some of the national offices have printed booklets for sale. The House of Lords Record Office publishes *A Short Guide to the Records of Parliament* and *Historic Parliamentary Documents*, and the Public Record Office has *Guides* and occasional catalogues for sale with illustrations of documents.

For illustrations the teacher must comb the illustrated books and periodicals listed in the *Guide to Illustrative Material for Use in Teaching History* (Historical Association), pp. 62-72. Children appreciate and understand history much more effectively if the subject can be visually illustrated. Some students and teachers imagine that a picture pinned to the wall is the answer to learning. Like every other aid, pictures can only assist understanding and have their limitations. However, in subjects such as social history, changes on the land, costume, transport, the army and navy and many other topics, pictures can be not only an invaluable aid to learning but a keen stimulation in themselves. A skilful teacher can, by using a Macmillan Class Picture with one or two documents, lead his class into a detailed analysis of a topic. Again, pictures can be the starting point for children's own artistic efforts, although pupils should very rarely be asked to 'copy' a picture. Much better, surely, to ask them to draw or paint another aspect of the story: a later stage of the battle; an 18th century farm as revealed by an enclosure map; a Victorian street scene, and so on. The conscientious teacher will, one hopes, acquire a portfolio of pictures as he proceeds and will use them as documents in their own right. If he is starting from scratch, however, there are various pictorial records available to him, and these are summarised in chapter 2. In general, paintings, drawings and etchings, especially of street scenes, are not difficult to find. The London Museum, for instance, publishes a good, short catalogue of drawings by Thomas Rowlandson, and these can be extremely useful if linked with

documents. Naturally, most suitable pictures are of the last two centuries and many will be in books, but one can easily have a photocopy made of a picture. Ideally, the teacher should have a ready supply of picture books in the classroom or the school library. In group work, one or two books will normally be sufficient to start children off on their own investigations.

Local collections of pictures are often held by public libraries and museums, and occasionally by record offices. Local professional photographers and postcard publishers sometimes have ancient pictures. Newspaper reports can be photocopied.

Otherwise, the British Museum has a wide collection of prints and drawings; the National Portrait Gallery, St Martin's Place, London, W.C.2, specialises in portraits of people of national interest, and at the same time the staff of the Gallery are compiling a record of family portraits. The National Maritime Museum, Greenwich, S.E.10, has pictures of ships, ports and sailors; the Science Museum, South Kensington, London, S.W.7, specialises in transport, engineering and industry; the Victoria and Albert Museum, South Kensington, London, S.W.7, has fine art pictures; and the Ministry of Public Building and Works, Lambeth Bridge House, London, S.E.1, has a wide range of prints of archaeological sites and buildings.

One should look upon pictures as essential documents, and if they can be linked with handwritten or printed documents in a scheme of work, with questionnaires and work-cards, the opportunities for using source material in class are greatly increased.

County Record Offices

For many teachers it might be best to begin with local records. These documents are readily available in county record offices and can be consulted on the spot. Suggestions for the use of documents in local history are contained in another chapter, but here we are concerned with the use of documents as a method of teaching in itself, and as a means of illustrating national issues.

In junior schools documents (or rather, facsimiles or photocopies) can serve as visual aids or as starting points for children's work on their own.[1] Pupils can construct their own documents with a rich variety of inks and coloured pencils, copy a page from the local Directory or draft

[1] *Archives and Source Material in the Junior School* by Joan E. Blyth, *Teaching History*, Vol.1, No. 1, 1969.

their own documents, given some information. The work is not very testing in terms of judgement and perception. However, documents can serve to stimulate the imagination, but in junior schools little else can be claimed for them.

In secondary schools there is more opportunity for work of greater depth. Children can look at different types of documents, read them, discuss their meaning, relate them to other events, answer questions in written or oral form, and indeed make some perceptive deductions from this evidence. The legibility of documents is of vital importance here, for the language of many manuscripts, quite apart from calligraphy, can present great problems.

There are guides and handbooks to help the teacher tackle the difficulties of handwriting. The WEA and the Extra-Mural Departments of universities often arrange evening classes in palaeography. F. G. Emmison's *Archives and Local History* (Methuen, 1966) is a good introduction, and other books mentioned elsewhere, especially John West's *Village Records* and the *Short Guides to Records*, edited by L. M. Munby and published for the Historical Association, are invaluable. Hilda Grieve's *Examples of English Handwriting, 1150–1750*, published by Essex County Council (2nd edition, 1959) gives help to those who wish to decipher the secretary hand and older forms of handwriting.

In preparing documents for use in schools, the county record offices have done pioneer work. The Essex County Record Office has been perhaps the main herald of these changes. At Ingatestone Hall a teaching and exhibition centre has been set up for the use of school-children and their teachers. Here, guided by a schools' archives officer, children can study and handle documents. At the Record Office there are opportunities for research by older children. Some of the local themes that have been studied are the development of the railways, the police, town histories, household management in the last two hundred years and similar topics. A variety of documents have been used for this purpose – inventories, wills, quarter sessions papers, parish registers, vestry minutes, school logbooks, militia papers and enclosure and tithe maps. The Essex County Record Office has also published a number of booklets, including *Georgian Essex*, *Victorian Essex* and *English History from Essex Sources* – all illustrated from county documents.

Some county record offices have made an effort to collect and edit documents on a local theme so that these source materials can be used in the classroom. Kent Archives Office, for instance, has produced some source books. Among them are *Some Roads and Bridges* and *Kent and the Civil War*. Cheap photocopying materials and facilities have meant that copies of documents can be everyday classroom aids. Kent Archives Office issues a catalogue of documents and Xerox copies can be ordered by schools. Gloucestershire Record Office has produced collections of documents for schools called *Signals* – Sources Illustrating Gloucestershire in National and Local History. Each *Signal* consists of photocopies of documents with explanatory notes for teachers. The two booklets completed are *The Cloth Industry in Gloucestershire, 1700–1840* and *Gloucestershire Turnpike Roads*. These booklets can be borrowed in sets of thirty by schools. One wishes that more record offices would follow the example of Essex, Kent and Gloucestershire.

Lancashire Records Office provides another valuable service by encouraging schoolchildren to visit the Office. Here a selection of documents based on a topic, place or period, at the teacher's request, are exhibited. In addition, the Record Office offers a sort of travelling exhibition. A member of the CRO staff travels to schools with portable showcases of documents and talks about them to children. The exhibitions may also be borrowed. Some of the titles in this series are *Shakespeare's Lancashire*, *Medieval Lancashire*, *Apprenticeship*, *The Civil War in Lancashire*, and so on. Valuable as this service is in allowing children to see original sources, the attitude of the pupils is again very often passive. In place of the teacher, someone else does the talking. The great advantage of the *Signals* and photocopies that are obtained by individual teachers is that they can be used by children directly, through work-cards or other schemes.

Consequently, there are three major ways in which county record offices can help schools. One is by arranging exhibitions, with perhaps a talk by the archivist or the schools' adviser, if the office has one. Here children are largely passive onlookers, unless the exhibition can be linked with work-sheets rather like those illustrated in the section on museum services.

A *Reward* notice, dated July 1864, shows how one district in Essex tackled the problem of crime detection; it serves as an example of the sort of document which may be used.

Burglary.

£10 REWARD

THE UNITED ASSOCIATION FOR THE PREVENTION OF CRIME AND PROSECUTION OF FELONS.

WHEREAS some Person or Persons did between the hours of Eleven and Four o'clock on the night of Monday the 18th July inst., enter the Dwelling-house called *Union Farm, West Hanningfield*, in the occupation of Mr. EDWARD SMITH, and STEAL therefrom

FOUR SILVER TABLE SPOONS,
TWO MARKED " A. C. C." and TWO MARKED "S."

4 SILVER DESSERT SPOONS,
MARKED "S."

1 PAIR PLATED NUTCRACKERS
1 PLATED BUTTER KNIFE,
1 PAIR SILVER SUGAR TONGS,
MARKED "S."

The Property of the said EDWARD SMITH, a member of the said Association.

Any Person giving such information as shall lead to the conviction of the Offender or Offenders, shall receive the above Reward—if more than one informant—the Reward to be apportioned.

W. W. DUFFIELD,
Secretary and Solicitor to the said Association.

CHELMSFORD, JULY 19, 1864.

JOHN DUTTON, PRINTER, CHELMSFORD.

A reward notice
By courtesy of Essex Record Office

Secondly, some archivists are willing to accept older children into the CRO to do some elementary research. Obviously this facility cannot be extended to younger children or large numbers of children, and therefore the applicants for research are largely sixth formers.

Thirdly, an increasing number of record offices go further and produce their own digests or collections for use in schools. This is the really valuable service, for photocopies of documents in the classroom allow the teacher scope to draft his own schemes of work and to involve children in practical activities. If county and city record offices and those who finance them could be encouraged to develop all three services for schools, but especially the last, teachers would be able to introduce more of this practical work into their lessons.

Seeing the urgent need for source material, other agencies have shown initiative in collecting it. The Institutes or Departments of Education of some universities have branched out into this field. The vanguard here was led by G. R. Batho of the University of Sheffield Institute of Education, who produced a number of folders of photocopied documents around Yorkshire themes. Among the titles are: *The Sheffield–Wakefield Turnpike Road*; *The Yorkshire Election of 1807*; *Parliamentary Elections*; *Barnsley in 1869*; *Mary, Queen of Scots in captivity*. In the folders are a number of photocopies of documents, engravings, portraits and large wall pictures, maps, diagrams and generous background notes for the teacher. Sets of these 'Archive Teaching Units', as they are called, can be borrowed by schools. One important feature of the Units is that they contain sufficient papers to allow children to work on their own.

The University of Newcastle Department of Education has followed a similar line with its Units. *Coals from Newcastle* has twenty-three documents and pictures for the study of the social and economic history of the North-East coalfield in the early 19th century. It also contains a reading list and suggestions for topic work. *Travel in the Turnpike Age* and *Railways in the Making* are two more titles in this series of Archive Teaching Units. At Worcester the initiative was taken by a group of teachers who selected documents from the CRO and local libraries to produce a series on *Worcestershire Roads*. One of the most encouraging signs of a renaissance in the teaching of history in recent years has been the emergence of local associations of history teachers. Some of these associations are producing Archive Teaching Units, and this will obviously greatly increase the numbers of these Units and will help to make them relevant to classroom use.

Other publications along a similar line but on a commercial basis are the *History at Source* volumes, published by Evans, under the editorship of J. M. Thomas. The first in the series, *Children 1773–1890* by Robert Wood, provides over fifty large facsimiles of original source material on this theme. There are advertisements, comics, criminal records, factory records, indentures, letters, pages from school books, posters, school reports and other documents. The second volume, *Roads before the Railways, 1700–1851* by J. M. Thomas contains a collection of large facsimiles of documents – posters, advertisements and news-sheets. Each volume is bound but may be taken apart so that illustrations can be used individually. There are no assignment sheets and if the teacher wishes to use the separate sheets in this way, he will have to write his own work-cards. However, this special binding means that teachers can dismantle the volume and use the documents for individual study purposes, group work or for display.

Other titles in the series include *Factory Life 1774-1885*; *Law and Order 1725–1866*; *Agriculture 1730–1872*; *Medicine 300–1929*; *Shopping 1721–1900*; *Scotland*; *The Rise of Cities 1703–1901*; *Entertainments 1800–1900*; *The Coming of the Railways 1813–1892*.

Another publisher, Macmillan, have published a series *Exploring History* which contains teaching kits on themes such as *The Navy*, *Homes*, *Law and Order* and *The Industrial Revolution*. These kits contain facsimiles of documents, pictures and assignment cards and are designed for individual and group work in the classroom.

Obviously, local record offices and university departments of education serve the local schools, whilst the *Jackdaws* deal in what might be called national topics. But what of the poor teacher whose school is situated in an area that does not possess such enterprising departments or offices? How does he employ documents? Apart from the published sources named in this chapter, he must cast around on his own to find material. One or two visits to the local record office, where he may find someone willing to co-operate in producing an Archive Teaching Unit, or if not where he will at least be able to select some documents for copying, is but a start. He must go on to look at the printed books in the local library, select pictures for copying, and begin to work out his projects or questionnaires for the children. Once he is launched he will discover that his dossier accumulates at an alarming rate. If he gains sufficient confidence in his own abilities to search for and compile his own material, he is on the way to becoming a much more stimulating and thoughtful schoolteacher. We have relied for too long on the textbook, which has eaten away at our enterprise. The chief difficulty is one not of opportunity, but of self-confidence.

References

Two articles that contain summaries of the main sources of archive kits are:

Fines J., *Archives in School, History*, October 1968

Jones G., and Watson D., *Archives in History Teaching – Some Problems, Teaching History*, Vol. 1, No. 3, 1970

Chapter Five

Local Sources and Children's Activities

Having examined the use of source material in schools and the practical schemes associated with local studies, we can now turn to the records themselves and begin to devise children's activities linked to them. Not all towns and villages will possess the records listed in this chapter, but teachers will be able to obtain photocopies and facsimiles of some of these documents. Once the selection has been made, the teacher has to guide children carefully, by setting specific tasks. Even Anglo-Saxon charters and the Domesday Survey can be used in this way, once the teacher has explained the meaning of the terms.

Anglo-Saxon charters

These charters recorded the conveyance of land in the period from 700 to 1066. They reveal details of land ownership after the Saxon invasions and give early evidence of place-names. The documents are in Latin and Anglo-Saxon but photocopies and a translation can easily be obtained. They are useful in the classroom primarily as visual illustrations. However, the translation can be put on to a stencil and used in the following ways.

1. Using the six-inch Ordnance Survey map, children can record any surviving landmarks named in the charter. The teacher will need to explain the purposes of the charter and any technical terms contained in it. J. West's *Village Records* and F. G. Emmison's *Archives and Local History* are useful here.

2. From the evidence on the charter, children can make their own maps of the charter bounds and compare these maps with the modern Ordnance Survey map of the same parish.

3. Using the Ordnance Survey map, and by taking an area covered by a six-mile radius from a village, children could study the place-names in this area, cataloguing them as field-names, forest-names, water-names and so on.

4. Children can construct their own charters on the pattern of the Anglo-Saxon charter, defining the bounds of the village, the town or the school. By careful draughtsmanship, with the use of coloured pencils or inks and sealing wax, the visual appearance of the 'charter' can be improved.

References

Cameron K., *English Place-Names*, Batsford, 1961

Ekwall E., *The Concise Oxford Dictionary of English Place-Names*, 4th edition, Oxford, The Clarendon Press, 1960

Gelling M., *Place-Names as Clues to History,* The Amateur Historian, Vol. 1, No. 2, 1952

Domesday Survey

The purpose of the Survey, ordered by William I at the Christmas meeting of the Royal Council at Gloucester in 1085, was to record the extent, wealth and feudal landholding of the Conqueror's new kingdom, and to assess land for tax purposes. The Survey was carried out by royal commissioners and local juries. The information describes manors and landholders before and after the Conquest, the taxable area of the manor in hides, the numbers of plough-teams belonging to both the lord of the manor and his tenants, and the number and social class of the villagers (mostly heads of the families only, so one must multiply by 4 or 5 to obtain the approximate population figure).

Again, a photograph or a photocopy is useful only as an illustration. However, the initiative

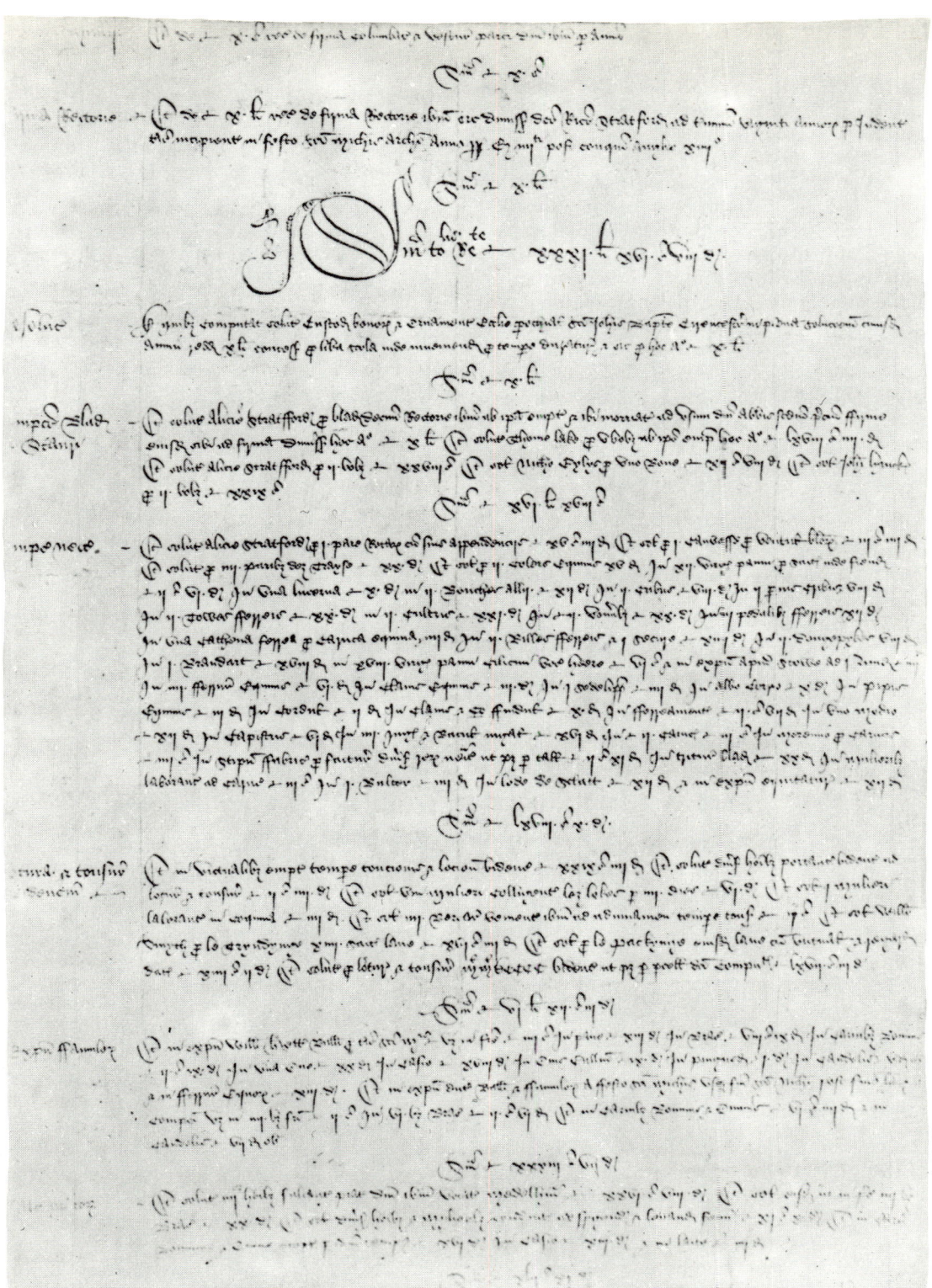

An Anglo-Saxon charter
Crown copyright

and imagination of children can be aroused by skilful use of a work-card.

1. Reading the extract from Domesday, children might draw a picture-map to include all the information given in the Survey.
2. Using the filmstrip *The Domesday Book*, the teacher should explain the history behind the Survey. One could attempt to match examples within the filmstrip with those contained in the Survey for the village.
3. A group of children could write a short play about the making of the village Domesday and then act it out with suitable 'props'.
4. Children could draw a map of the county (or a smaller area) to show the lands held by the different landowners named in the Survey. (The *VCH* normally gives these details.)
5. The Domesday Survey can be used to introduce Norman England, the Conquest, the Bayeux Tapestry and the rule of William I.

Filmstrips

The Bayeux Tapestry, Parts 1/2, Visual Productions, LH1/LH2, 1967
England at the Time of the Conquest, VP, LH3, 1967
Edgar the Saxon, Hulton, 1958
The Domesday Book, Unicorn Head, 1951

References

Ballard A., *The Domesday Inquest*, Methuen, 1906
Bedford Franklin T., *Domesday*, Amateur Historian, Vol. 1, No. 9, 1953–54 (3 articles)
Galbraith V. H., *The Making of Domesday Book*, OUP, 1961
Welldon-Finn R., *The Domesday Inquest*, Longmans, 1961
Welldon-Finn R., *Domesday Book*, Jackdaw No. 39, Cape

An extract from the Domesday Survey of Gloucestershire.

Translation

IV Land of the Church of Hereford

In Cheltenham hundred the Bishop of Hereford held Prestbury. There are thirty hides. There are three ploughs in the demesne; and eighteen villeins and five bordars and nine ploughs. There is a priest and one radknight with two ploughs; and in Winchcombe one burgess pays eighteen-pence; and eleven bondmen and bondwomen; there are twenty acres of meadow, and a wood of one mile long and a half broad.

To this manor belongs one vill, Sevenhampton, out of this hundred. There are twenty of the above mentioned thirty hides; and there are two ploughs there; and twenty-one villeins with eleven ploughs. Of these twenty hides Durand holds three hides of the bishop.

The whole manor was in King Edward's time worth twelve pounds; now sixteen pounds. Robert, the bishop of the same city, holds this manor.

Gloucester Domesday Survey
Crown copyright

Medieval life

Many aspects of everyday life in the town and countryside may be illustrated from documents. A medieval court roll or deed with heraldic symbols may stimulate children's interest and awaken dormant energies. Documents of a much later date may of course illustrate medieval customs, and even mid-18th century maps of open fields, town plans and manor court regulations are useful for this purpose.

The manor

Most manors were roughly the same size as the parish, until in the later middle ages some very large manors became subdivided. Each lord of the manor held regular courts which the tenants were obliged to attend. The business dealt with in such courts largely related to land tenure, dues and services, petty crime and local administration. The earliest court rolls recording these affairs date from the late 13th century and provide a picture of work in the medieval manor. In the classroom the teacher will have to explain the functions of the manor, its court and its customs. Once this has been done, children can be set various tasks.

1. Using a document from a manor court roll, such as the one relating to Sherborne, children can be asked to write a class play on the theme of the *Manor Court*, with villeins accused of offences such as theft of corn or beasts, wrongfully raising the hue and cry, beating servants, allowing cattle to roam on a neighbour's land, and so on.
2. Here is a typical extract from a manor court roll: 'John Brooke, because he stole a cow belonging to Margery Clarke and detained the same against his word. Pledge John Pictor. Fine sixpence'.
Children can be set tasks such as drawing a picture of John Brooke's appearance in court, making up a story on the same theme, and explaining the words 'pledge' and 'fine'.
3. Using illustrations contained in the Macmillan *History Class Pictures*, set drawing, painting and writing exercises based on the separate pictures. There are reference books linked to the pictures which give clues.

Filmstrips

The Medieval Manor, EP, 1950
Piers the Villein, Unicorn Head, 1950
Illustrations of life from the Luttrell Psalter, Rank, 1948

The Village, Common Ground, 1950
Medieval Britain, 3 parts, VP, 1965
Sixteenth Century Occupations, Hulton, 1950
Life in the Middle Ages, Hulton, 1951

References

Hilton R. H., *Life in the Medieval Manor*, Amateur Historian, Vol. 1, No. 3, 1953
Latham R. E., *Coping with Medieval Latin*, Amateur Historian, Vol. 1, No. 3, 1954
Latham L. C., *The Manor and the Village*, in *Social Life in Early England*, Historical Association 1960
Hone N. J., *The Manor and Manorial Records*, Methuen, 1906
Bennett H. S., *Life on the English Manor*, CUP, 1956.

A Manor Court Roll

The Sherborne Muniments, September 1484 – September 1485

The original document is useful only as an illustration. But using the translation, children can be asked questions or set assignments similar to these.

1. What are 'victuals'? Draw up a list of items of food and drink that might have been consumed by the people working on this estate.
2. Why did the manor court employ a priest, Brother Lenche, to serve as its clerk?
3. Richard Smyth was paid 16s. 4d. for 'le Tryndynge'. By reading the previous and subsequent entries on the preparation of wool, explain what you think the term means.
4. What evidence is there to indicate that this was a most prosperous estate?
5. Draw or paint a picture of the manor court in session, showing the table, the clerk, the steward, and servants waiting to be paid. Try to make the costume and furnishings as accurate as possible, using any available reference material.

Parish records

The ecclesiastical parish dates from Saxon times, and from about 1550 the Crown delegated many responsibilities to county and parish officials. The records of the parish may include registers of baptisms, marriages and burials; churchwardens' accounts for the maintenance of the church; vestry minutes on the care of the poor; highways; accounts and papers of the overseers of the poor relating to relief, resettlement and movement of the poor; and accounts of the surveyors of the highways. There may also be papers about parish charities, schools, the parsonage, parish surveys

	£ s. d.	£ s. d.	
PAYMENTS. Brought forward	... ...	30 6 10	Brother Lenche's Account.

4.—Washing and Shearing of Sheep :—

	£ s. d.	£ s. d.
For Victuals bought during the washing and shearing	1 9 4	
To men for carrying the sheep at the washing and shearing	0 2 4	
To a woman collecting the fleeces for four days	0 0 6	
To a woman working in the kitchen ...	0 0 4	
To four shepherds for coming and assisting at shearing time	0 2 0	
To Richard Smyth for 'le Tryndynge' fourteen sacks of wool	0 16 4	
For packing said wool, with victuals and wages given	0 14 2	
For washing and shearing 2,900 sheep, as appears by parcel of said Account ...	3 7 3	
		6 12 3

5.—Expenses of Servants :—

For Expenses of William Heriett, Bailiff, for the term of St Michael, as follows :—

	£ s. d.	£ s. d.
For Corn	0 4 0	
„ Bread	0 1 1	
„ Malt	0 8 9	
„ Carcases of Oxen	0 2 9	
„ 1 Sheep	0 1 8	
„ Cheese	0 1 6	
„ Hens' eggs	0 0 9	
„ Lard	0 0 1	
„ Candles	0 0 5	
„ Shoeing of horses	0 1 1	

Expenses of said Bailiff and Servants as follows :—

	£ s. d.	£ s. d.
For 4 Bushels of Corn	0 2 0	
„ 6 Bushels of Malt	0 2 6	
„ Carcases of Oxen and Sheep ...	0 6 4	
„ Candles	0 0 7	1 13 *7
Carried forward		£38 12 8

* Brother Lenche's sum is in error here. The pence should be 6d.

Brother Lenche's accounts
By courtesy of Lord Sherborne

with enclosure and tithe maps, and possibly militia papers.

Only in rare circumstances will all these papers be available, but for the ones which are, most will be of the late 17th century onwards; reading is therefore not too difficult, although spelling is very often eccentric.

Children's work

1. Children can write short stories or biographies about the lives of the villagers – the weaver, the inn-keeper, the constable, the vagabond, the Catholic priest on the run, the pedlar and the parson.
2. Using suitable filmstrips such as: *Tudor Life*, Common Ground, 1949; *Seventeenth Century Occupations*, Picture Post, 1950; *The Evolution of the English Parish Church*, CG, 1955; or *Life in Tudor Times*, Common Ground, 1964; the teacher can describe the background to parish records and can stimulate project or group work on 'Life in the 16th and 17th centuries'.
3. The records can be used to initiate work on the village church – its architecture, furnishings, former parsons, lands and so on.

References

Brinkworth E. R. C., *Evidence from Ecclesiastical Sources*, three articles in Amateur Historian, 1954–5
Ketchley C. P., *Practical Work on the Parish Chest*, Amateur Historian, Vol. 2, No. 3, 1954–5
Tate W. E., *The Parish Chest*, CUP, 1960
Tupling G. H., *Searching the Parish Records*, six articles in Amateur Historian, 1953–4

Tithe apportionments and maps

From 787 onwards, compulsory tithes (one tenth of all produce) were levied by the Church on the laity. In the 18th century the opposition of farmers occasionally led to the substitution of a money rent or an allotment of land on enclosure instead of a tithe of produce.

In 1836 the Tithe Commutation Act replaced all payments in kind by money rents, and in the following years most parishes were surveyed, mapped and apportionments of land allocated. These maps give details of land ownership, land usage and other details, and can usefully be compared with the enclosure maps.

Filmstrips

Turnip Townsend's Ploughboy, Hulton, 1958
The Agrarian and Industrial Revolution, EP, 1961
Agriculture and the Land, in 2 parts, Common Ground, 1949
How to look at a Village, Common Ground, 1947

Reference

Tupling G. H., *Tithe and Enclosure Awards*, Amateur Historian, Vol. 1, No. 12, 1954

Turnpike roads, canals and railways

In 1555 the parish was made responsible for the main roads between market towns, and accounts by surveyors of the highways may therefore be found among parish records. Throughout the 18th century many more turnpike trusts were established by Acts of Parliament. The plans of these roads, bridges and diversions, if extant, are usually to be found in the CRO together with the minutes and accounts of some of the Trusts. The documents can be usefully employed to throw light on road-building in this period, both in the county and on a national scale.

The canals of the 18th and early 19th centuries were also planned to meet the demand for better communications, particularly for the carriage of heavy goods, such as coal and textiles. The printed Acts of Parliament and plans of the canals are often to be found in the CRO. Otherwise, the archives may be in the British Transport Historical Records Office, 66 Porchester Road, London, W.2.

The archives of the former railway companies are at the British Transport Historical Records Office, and so unless he visits London, the teacher is limited to printed sources, such as newspaper reports, the standard histories of the companies, and plans of proposed railways, many of which were never constructed. Railways (deserted, closed or operative) awaken perennial interest in children and the combination of some documents, illustrations from the local museum, picture books and a visit or two can result in children's work of high calibre.

Children's work

1. With turnpike maps, it is not difficult to compare the map with a modern OS map, identifying and colouring in the turnpike road. This exercise can lead on to the study of the modern OS map and its symbols. Again, children can be asked to list the new buildings and the roads built since the original turnpike was constructed.
2. If the turnpike road is nearby, the map can serve as a guide to fieldwork, so that the children might be able to follow the course of the road on the ground. It is not difficult to note places where the turnpike road has been improved and altered since its inception. If there were toll-houses in the

past, they might be identified then and sketched.

3. Children could be set tasks on the road-makers – Metcalf, Telford and Macadam. If these or other famous engineers have worked locally try to find out details of the bridges, roads or canals they built.

4. Read extracts from *Nicholas Nickleby, Tom Brown's Schooldays* or *Pickwick Papers* of coach-rides in this period. Pupils might write imaginative accounts of a coach-ride from London to one's own town or village in the late 18th century.

5. Children could sketch, draw or paint pictures of aspects of roadbuilding – the navvies at work, toll-houses or toll-gates, a coach waylaid by highwaymen and so on.

6. Similarly, work which involves the use of documents, maps and imaginative composition, both written and visual, can be applied to canals and railways.

7. This material gives the teacher an opportunity to set up schemes of individual and class study – projects on canals, roads, railways; model-making; scrapbooks; friezes; painting and drawing.

Filmstrips:

Land Transport, Common Ground, 1949
The Evolution of British Railways, BT, 1959
Transport in the 18th Century, Common Ground, 1965
Roads, Rivers and Canals, Common Ground, 1949
Railways, Ships and Trade, Common Ground, 1949
The History of Road Transport, 3 parts, Common Ground, 1949
Early Locomotives, Unicorn, 1950

References:

Cossons A., *Misconceptions about Turnpikes*, Amateur Historian, Vol. 5, No. 2, 1962
French E. C. W., *Turnpike Trusts*, Amateur Historian, Vol. 2, No. 1, 1954

Brasses

Monumental brasses can be found in over three thousand English churches and cathedrals, ranging from the 13th century to the 18th century. They can be of immense value in teaching local history, costume and medieval warfare, and they are as valuable as printed documents in providing children with ideas.

There are a number of books on brasses, brass-rubbing and the techniques of this kind of study.

A selection of the most useful titles follow:

Notes on Brass-rubbing, Oxford University Archaeological Society, Ashmolean Museum, Oxford, 1967
Discovering Monumental Brasses, Shire Publications, 1966
Mann J. G., *Monumental Brasses*, Penguin, 1957

The increasing popularity of brass-rubbing as a hobby and the fragile nature of the brasses have forced many clergymen to forbid children from making rubbings. However, wherever possible, children should be encouraged to go on brass-rubbing expeditions, either as a class venture or privately. The permission of the local parson must always be obtained and often there is a small fee charged.

The technique of brass-rubbing is fairly easy to master but the teacher would be well advised to obtain the proper materials – heelball or wax, white rag paper, sellotape, a soft brush and a duster. Firms that specialise in the supply of this equipment are:

Philipps and Page Ltd., 50 Kensington Church Street, London, W.8
Alec Tiranti Ltd., 72 Charlotte Street, London, W.1

It is not difficult to obtain positive prints of a brass-rubbing. This can be done by photographing the rubbing, and by making a positive print from the negative. One often sees in the classroom a superb rubbing made by the teacher and used as an illustration. That is one function, but there are many others.

1. One can encourage children to make their own rubbings and then to colour them with coloured pencils or paint. The costume, armour and weapons of the figures can be compared with other illustrations from books or postcards. In this way children can be drawn on to investigate medieval dress, warfare, heraldry, genealogy and other topics.

2. The brasses can be used as models for work in other materials: clay, plasticine, lino-cut patterns and paintings.

3. From the brasses the class can go on to project work on the tournament, chivalry, warfare, costume and the history of the families illustrated in the rubbings.

4. The filmstrip, *The Colour of Chivalry* (Educational Productions, 1950), has colourful illustrations taken from brasses and effigies and can be used to stimulate children's drawing and painting.

Gloucester 5th. May 1828.

Dear Sir,

I beg leave to state, that I have this day inspected the Over Bridge Works, and seen the Centers relieved from the Masonry of the Arch, every thing stands in a perfect State, and I am justified in declaring the whole, as regard materials and workmanship, fully equal to any thing of the kind in Europe. —

I remain Yours very sincerely

Thos. Telford

To. Edward Bloxsome Esqr.
    Clerk of the Peace

A letter from Telford
By courtesy of Gloucestershire County Council

Bridge at Over, Gloucestershire

Thomas Telford was called upon in May 1828 to inspect a bridge at Over, Glos., which he had constructed some time earlier. He was proud of his own work and described the bridge as 'fully equal to anything of the kind in Europe'.

Quarter Sessions papers

The courts of the Quarter Sessions were the major instruments of local administration from Tudor times to the late 19th century. The magistrates were responsible for maintaining law and order and the affairs of local government. Crime and punishment, highways and bridges, the licensing of inns, enclosure, the poor, prisons, registration of nonconformist meeting houses, the registering of electors – these were some of the matters dealt with by the justices. Very often one comes across papers submitted to the justices on the number of alehouses in the village, the manufacture of wool, hides and tobacco, the use of inns for gambling, vagrancy, enclosures and local militia musters.

Children's work

1. Here is an extract from some Quarter Sessions papers of a Worcestershire village, quoted by John West in *Village Records*, p. 87. The date is 1615.
'Articles concerning the misdemeanour of Margaret Bache, wife of John Bache, Nailer, a common scold. She is a source of strife amongst her neighbours, and has been presented as a scold at the Leate holden for the Manor of Chaddesley. She was also presented at a visitation at Bromsgrove for "misbehaving her tongue against her mother-in-law", in October 1603, and excommunicated.'

Children might be asked these questions:

(a) Explain the meaning of the words: scold, Leate, excommunicated.
(b) Write an account, with dialogue, of the trial of Margaret Bache.
(c) Write out the speech of the justices, giving their punishment.
(d) Draw a picture to illustrate the trial. Make the costumes and settings as accurate as possible by studying picture books.

Reference

Emmison F. G. and Gray I., *County Records*, Historical Association, 1961

Application by Mary Browning for Poor Law Relief, 1803.

Gloucestershire C.R.O.

This application is typical of many such documents to be found in Quarter Sessions' papers. If it can be read by pupils, the application can serve as an introduction to the Poor Law, poverty, village life in the early 19th century and more topics such as these. However, there is more to this particular application than first meets the eye. Mary Browning's first husband, Samuel Bird, probably died in the campaigns in Egypt. This link with the 28th Regiment of Foot, later to form part of the Gloucestershire Regiment, adds a little spice to the story, which is sad and amusing enough in itself. Arising from this single document are a number of questions. We do not know all of the answers but children can be encouraged to think about the problems, make assumptions and carry on investigations through printed books.

The teacher should perhaps preface the use of the application by saying something about the objectives of the Poor Law and the machinery of dispensation – application to the Justices, the levy from the rates, the grants of money to paupers outside the workhouse – and the depression within the Gloucestershire wool industry caused by the wars with France at the turn of the century. Or children can be asked to find out the answers to these questions by looking up the facts in books.

A work-card or questionnaire might be phrased rather like this:

Read this application and answer the questions.

1. Write down several reasons why you think Mary Browning is applying for Poor Law relief (you will have to guess at some of the reasons).
2. Write down the speech of one of the Justices, giving his award.
3. Rodborough and Stroud, where Mary Browning lived, were centres of the Gloucestershire woollen industry. One of the reasons for Mary's poverty may have been that she and her second husband were unemployed. Find out as much as you can about the wool industry at this time and write down the reasons for its decline in 1803.
4. We do not know for sure what happened to Samuel Bird. However, the 28th Regiment of Foot which later became the Gloucestershire Regiment served in Egypt in 1801 and took part in the campaigns against the French. Here is an

Gloucestershire
to wit

The Examination of Mary Browning otherwise Bird now residing in the parish of Rodborough in the said County taken on her Oath before us two of his Majesty's Justices of the peace in and for the said County the ninth day of November 1803 Who on her oath saith that she was born in the parish of Stroud in the said County that about nine Years ago she was Married to Samuel Bird of the parish of Stroud aforesaid Shearman by whom she had one child named Samuel now of the age of Eight Years that about three Quarters of a Year after she was Married to the said Samuel Bird he the said Samuel Bird went away from her and she never heard any thing from him for about three Years and then she had two Letters saying that he was dead that about two Years after this Examinant heard that the said Samuel Bird was dead she then Married to Charles Browning of the parish of Rodborough aforesaid by whom she had one Child namely Martha now of the age of about four Years and an half but about three Weeks after she was delivered of the said last mentioned Child her Husband Samuel Bird returned home to her and stayed about one Week and he then went away and she hath never seen him since but she saith that she hath heard that he died in Egypt that she still continued living with the said Charles Browning by whom she hath had one other child named John now of the age of about two Years and an half And this Examinant further saith that her said three Children were all born in the Parish of Rodborough aforesaid and she further saith that she hath not done any act of her own Knowledge whereby to gain a Settlement out of the said Parish of Stroud

Sworn before us,   the mark of
J. Hawkins
                                                    Mary Browning otherwise Bird

The examination of Mary Browning
By courtesy of Rodborough Parish Council

extract from a book about the Regiment's history:

'In March 1801 the 28th Regiment of Foot sailed for Egypt as part of a combined operation by the Navy and 15,000 troops against Napoleon's "Army of the East". The Army came ashore under heavy fire from the French and on March 21 1801 fought a major battle some six miles from Alexandria. The 28th held a key position at the pivot of the British line; four French columns were flung against the 28th, which withstood one attack after another, standing shoulder to shoulder in two ranks. For four hours the 28th repulsed first infantry and then cavalry assaults.

The French commander tried a different ruse. He sent two regiments of dragoons up a valley and swung them around to fall on the 28th's rear. Lt.Col. Chambers commanded his troops: "Rear rank, 28th! Right About Face!" This turned the rear rank about, to stand back to back with their fellows in the front rank. A series of musket volleys cut holes in the ranks of the charging French cavalry. However, the French launched a number of charges, riding in three ranks, close together, with men leaning over their horses' necks, sabres at the ready. The 28th's muskets stopped every charge, and their drawn bayonets finished off the few daring Frenchmen who reached the British ranks.

In common with other regiments which fought in Egypt, the 28th was granted the special honour of bearing the Sphinx and the word "Egypt" on their colours, but they were also granted the unique privilege of wearing the regimental number on the back of their head-dress, as well as on the front, a reminder of their famous action at Alexandria.'[1]

Write an imaginary account of the adventures of Samuel Bird, after he left home to join the Regiment. Describe his soldiering, his return, the shock of finding his wife married again and his subsequent flight back to the Army and his part in the campaign in Egypt which led to his death. Illustrate your answer with drawings or paintings if you wish.

Maps
Estate maps
Estate maps were developed from written surveys in late Tudor times, though most surviving ones date from about 1700 to 1850. They vary enormously in accuracy and the amount of detail

[1] Daniell, D. S., *Cap of Honour : The Story of the Gloucestershire Regiment*, 1694–1950, Harrap, 1951.

shown on them, but most show open or enclosed fields, place-names, buildings, roads, and land use. After 1840 estate maps were often based on tithe maps. In the classroom they are useful for visual reasons, for very often the maps show woodland, villages, houses, bridges, roads and pathways, often with illustrations in water-colours. Children can be set tasks such as examining the lands held by individual landowners, the common-land, field-names and the routes of roads.

Reference:
Harley J. B., *Maps for the Local Historian*, Amateur Historian, 1967–8

County maps
County maps are extremely useful as a means of comparison with modern OS maps and most CROs have collections of maps which can be photocopied. Most of the 16th and 17th century maps show relief, forests, parks, bridges, towns and villages, and they can be useful in the classroom as visual aids.

Enclosure
The enclosure of the open fields has been a gradual process since the middle ages, but there are few accessible maps recording enclosure before the age of parliamentary enclosure in the late 18th and early 19th centuries. Acts of Parliament, Commissioners' minutes, awards and maps with related papers concerning the final enclosures of the last of the open fields and commons are the documents studied by historians. The information provided by the awards and maps relates principally to the old open field agriculture, land ownership and occupation, and the formation of modern farms. Very often there is also evidence of field-names, glebe lands, roads, footpaths and boundaries.

Children's work
1. Make a study (with a map) of a modern farm, recording information such as land-use, land ownership, crops, roads and field-names. Compare the results with the enclosure map.
2. If the maps are available, compare a 16th century map with the enclosure map and this with the modern six-inch OS map. Find out, on the ground, what has happened to the common land, the land formerly owned by the church, the manorial estates and the major landowners in the 16th and late 18th centuries.

3. List the various field-names and try to find evidence, both on the map and on the ground, of ridge and furrow, field boundaries, strip cultivation.

References

Coppock J. T., *Changes in Form and Field Boundaries*, Amateur Historian, Vol. 3, No. 7, 1958

Franklin T. B., *Enclosures in the 19th century*, Amateur Historian, Vol. 1, No. 6, 1953

Mayne L. B., *Maps from Saxton to Royal Ordnance*, Amateur Historian, Vol. 1, No. 12, 1954

Hoskins W. G., *The Midland Peasant*, Macmillan, 1957

Parker R. A. C., *Enclosures in the 18th Century*, Aids for Teachers series, Historical Association, No. 7, 1960

Chambers J. D. and Mingay G. E., *The Agricultural Revolution, 1750–1880*, Batsford, 1966

Phillips C. W., *A Guide to Ordnance Survey Maps as Historical Sources*, Amateur Historian, Vol. 5, No. 6, 1963

The Historian's Guide to Ordnance Survey Maps, The National Council of Social Service, 1965

Inventories and wills

Until 1858 wills had to be proved in ecclesiastical courts. This was normally done in the bishops' consistory courts unless the deceased person had property in two or more dioceses. Original wills are kept at Somerset House, London, W.C.2, but many counties have a calendar of wills. These documents contain evidence about property, charities, personal possessions, furniture and kitchen utensils, and they can be extremely valuable for illustrating social history. The inventories that accompanied the wills often list jewellery, clothes, farming tools and stock, debts and trading equipment. The documents are usually not difficult to read, although the spelling might present some amusing problems.

Inventories should be closely linked to museum exhibits, or pictures of furniture and household effects. If the evidence is visual, children can see clearly the changing fashions and styles. The Geffrye Museum, for instance, produces excellent little books on *English Homes*, outline books on *Furniture, Costume, Doors, Windows and Walls*, and information books on *Furniture* and other topics. The Museum of English Rural Life at Reading has postcards of farm tools and domestic furnishings. Other folk museums, principally at Bristol, Bradford, Cardiff, Barnard Castle (Durham), Gloucester, Shibden Hall (Halifax), the Victoria and Albert Museum (London) and the Castle Museum at York sell postcards and pamphlets suitable for this type of work in schools.

Children's work

1. Children might be encouraged to collect pictures of furniture and to illustrate every item in an inventory.

2. One can compare the contents of a room, say a kitchen or a dining room, in an 18th century house with the same rooms of a pupil's house today.

3. If the house mentioned in the inventory is still standing, try to gain admission and compare the furnishings today with those detailed in the inventory.

Filmstrips

18th Century Occupations, Hulton, 1951
Social Life in the 18th Century, Hulton, 1951

References

Steer F. W., *Probate Inventories*, in Short Guides to Records, Historical Association.

Ashmore O. and Bagley J. J., *Inventories as a Source of Local History*, four articles in the Amateur Historian, 1959–60

Inventory of a house, Tyrol Villa, at Cheltenham, Glos., 1871.

This extract from an inventory of a large house gives an indication of how a document can be used to introduce a topic such as 'the Victorians at home'. Inventories should be used in conjunction with illustrated books, such as those published by the Geffrye Museum; a selection of titles has been listed above.

Children's work

1. Draw the following objects found in this Victorian house: a sofa; a cane-bottomed chair; a curved music-stand; a French clock; a foot stool; a glass chandelier; a bead bag; a brass trivet; an ottoman.

2. Make a collection of pictures and drawings of Victorian furniture and houses.

3. Make two lists:
(a) of items found in Tyrol Villa and not found in a house today; (b) items listed in Tyrol Villa which are found in houses today.

4. How did the Victorians light and heat their homes?

If the inventory can be used in conjunction with a picture of a Victorian interior, more imaginative

A Victorian Inventory
By courtesy of Gloucestershire County Council

work can be set. The picture of a Victorian kitchen, linked to the inventory, tells more about the life of a middle class family than long explanations.

A Victorian Kitchen

On page 56 is a picture of a kitchen built into the basement of a large house. The family who owned the house would have been fairly wealthy. The father might have been a millowner, a prosperous merchant or a solicitor.

Children's work

1. What form of lighting was used in this house?
2. The cook did her cooking on the 'kitchen range'. Name the different parts of the range (oven, hob, etc.), and make out a menu for the meal being served by the maid. What evidence is there to show that this family liked heavy, substantial meals?
3. Name the objects marked A, B and C.
4. To the right of the fireplace hangs a revolving meat jack. The meat hung from a hook attached to a revolving wheel which turned the meat as it roasted in front of the fire; below it was a dish to catch the fat. Design and illustrate with sketches two other pieces of kitchen equipment: a toaster and a griller.
5. Draw a picture of a scene in a Victorian dining-room. Try to make the clothes of the family and the servants, the furniture and decorations as accurate as you can by looking at pictures in books.

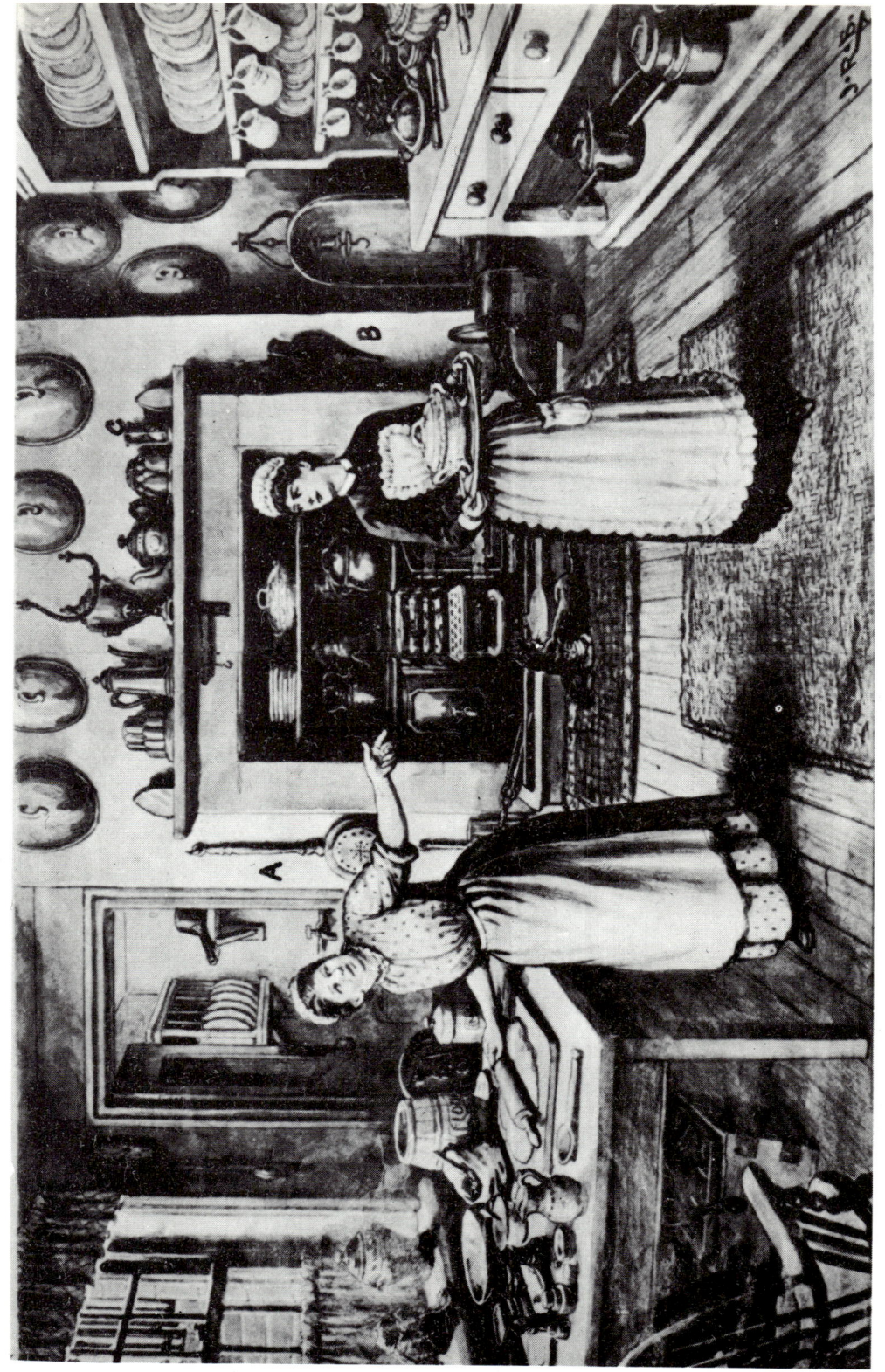

A Victorian kitchen
By courtesy of the editor of Pictorial Education

56

Town development in the 19th century

The vast growth of the modern town in the last century offers many opportunities for work in the classroom and outside it. The geographical enlargement of towns can best be seen by children from maps, sale particulars, newspapers and the commercial directories. The improvement of public services can be seen in the Acts of Parliament and plans in the CRO, but they may well be too dry and legal for class use. The records of the Town Commissioners, Boards of Health, Sanitary Authorities and District Councils are usually able to be seen and photocopied at the local CRO or at the Town Hall, and these papers provide amusing and relevant information on the development of the town.

There are many aspects of town life that one can study through documents, pictures and books. Some of these subjects lend themselves to class teaching – the coming of the railways, crime and punishment, the poor, prisons and local schools, for instance. Otherwise for group, individual or class studies there are subjects such as working conditions, transport, trade unions, wages, local industries, clothing, furniture, houses and parliamentary elections. For all these subjects there will be documents in the County Record Office, books in the City or Town library and pictures in the museum, all of which offer opportunities to awaken interest, develop subjects in depth and provide children with practical, meaningful learning.

Children's work

1. One can try to interest children in projects which construct a picture of town life a hundred years ago. Models, friezes, street plans, maps, scrapbooks of town life, imaginary newspaper accounts and topics such as houses, shops, crime, schools and roads can all be investigated and developed.

2. Children can construct an imaginary town newspaper on the lines of the *Historical News Sheets* published by Allen and Unwin. Pupils can devise articles on sport, news, fashion, politics, overseas news and so on, illustrating the 'newspaper' with advertisements, sketches and drawings.

3. Some fieldwork can be attempted by using an extract from a 19th century Directory as a guide to a town or village. Children can be asked to investigate surviving streets, shops, houses, trades and the family names of the proprietors.

4. One can start a class museum on Victoriana, using family photographs, old books and objects brought from home by the children. Ask pupils to talk about the exhibit that they bring to school.

Filmstrips

English Houses through the Ages, Hulton, 1950
English Costume, Common Ground, 1954
Furnishings (in five parts), Tartan, 1954
The Kitchen through the Ages, Hulton, 1951
Social Life in the 19th Century (in two parts), Rank, 1949
Victorian Social Life, Hulton, 1950
The End of the Victorian Era, EP, 1967

Chapter Six

The Museum and the School

In any practical work-scheme for children, the local museum should play an integral part. Fortunately, museums are becoming more and more alive to the needs of the schools and are adapting their collections to an active, junior audience rather than the occasional adult visitor on a wet afternoon.

The ideal situation for a teacher to enjoy would be to establish contacts with a museum or gallery which works closely with a local teachers' organisation or which has a Schools' Officer solely responsible for work with teachers and pupils. If the expertise of the museum staff, who are aware of the visual and cultural value of the exhibits, can be linked to the teacher's skill in adapting these objects to children's needs, the schools can gain tremendous value from the museum services.

Services

What are these services that the museum has to offer? If a teacher is fortunate in having a local museum or gallery within reach he might begin by asking the following questions.

Visits: Does this museum cater for children's visits? Does it have a Schools' Officer? Do the staff provide illustrated talks? Do they have a published list of titles of these talks? Are the talks suitable for primary, as well as secondary schools?

Exhibits: Are the exhibits shown in periods (Roman Britain, the Age of Victoria, etc.) or by subjects (furniture, portraits, jewellery)? If there is a lecture-tour, is it merely a general tour of the display rooms, in which miscellaneous objects are described? If so, this type of lecture is to be avoided, for the lecturer may not be able to gauge the mental ability of his audience and so pitch his talk at too high or too low a level. Secondly, if thirty or more children are grouped around one case, only a handful will actually see the exhibit and hear the remarks.

Children's work: Does the museum provide the children with work-cards, folders or question-naires? Are the questions suitable for the age and ability of the children in your class? Does the museum possess a classroom where exhibits, slides, filmstrips and films can be shown by a member of the museum's staff?

Aids: Does the museum have printed guide-books, pamphlets, post-cards, photographs and slides for sale? Is there a museum loan-service? If the answer to the majority of these questions is 'Yes', the museum to which it refers is to be warmly congratulated.

An organisation, *The Group for Educational Services in Museums* (Secretary, City Museum, Queen's Road, Bristol 8), co-ordinates the various activities of the museums in Great Britain which do offer help to teachers, students and others engaged in education. The museums listed on page 62-3 are not the only museums in Great Britain, but they are singled out by the Group as institutions which offer substantial help to teachers. These services cover the loan of material for use in the classroom, exhibitions in school or college, guided tours or talks in the galleries, museum lessons, work-sheets or questionnaires for children visiting the museum, film shows and model-making. Not all museums can offer all these services and no two museums are totally alike in the assistance they offer. A selection of the services offered by museums is given at the end of this chapter, but teachers should write to the Organiser of the Service in their area for full details of the Service.

Children's visits to museums

The *objectives* of a visit may be:

to illustrate a series of lessons on the Romans in Britain, country life in the 18th century, or a dozen such topics that might be illustrated by a visit to a gallery or museum;
to apply local archaeological evidence to a class lesson, such as one on the Iron Age;
to form part of a study of local history;
to illustrate a class project, for instance furniture, transport or dress.

Whatever the objective of the visit, it ought to add colour, excitement and insight to the study of history. A visit should be an educational experience, training eyes to see and minds to judge. Out of this training one hopes to encourage critical assessment and a deeper appreciation of the richness of the cultural heritage.

However, if children are to gain the maximum advantage from a visit to a museum, they should be properly prepared. Children of all ages and abilities will work voluntarily and amazingly hard if they are given the right incentives. A visit should never be merely a jaunt, a change from the regularity of class lessons or an occasion for passive observation. It should be part of a scheme of work, linked by work-cards or questionnaires to activities in the classroom. In short, it should be a practical activity.

Classroom preparation

It would be wise to do some preliminary classroom teaching before a visit. This might take the following forms:

Teachers might make a reconnaissance visit to the museum. This gives the teacher the opportunity to discover details of the museum's geography and services, and allows him to construct a work-card.

Some background information should be given in class. If the children are already studying Roman Britain and the objective of the visit is to investigate the Roman occupation in a particular part of the country, the preparation obviously need not be extensive, but it should at least set the scene.

Children should be made aware, even in a sketchy way, of how the objects were discovered and how archaeologists work. They should know, for instance, that our understanding of life in the Bronze or Stone Age is based upon fragments, and it is these fragments that they are going to see for themselves.

At this stage, children should be given clear instructions on behaviour in the museum. Most objects will be behind glass, but some may not be and one must assume that they are fragile. However, if the work is properly organised, the children should behave as normally as they do in the classroom.

Working models are sometimes demonstrated to children, and the teacher should discover if there is anything of this nature, a spinning jenny for instance, which can be shown to children. Sometimes museums allow pupils to handle exhibits such as flints, domestic utensils and models.

Work-sheets

By far the best way of ensuring that children use a museum is by providing them with work-sheets or questionnaires. This is not to say that there is no educational value in aimlessly walking around a gallery but in general children will gain greater insight if their viewing is directed. In two museums in particular, the Geffrye in London and the City of Liverpool, children's visits have been carefully and brilliantly organised. Other museums provide talks, conducted tours, loans, classroom illustrations and printed books but few offer printed questionnaires. Consequently, the enterprising teacher will want to construct his own work-card. Where does he start?

In devising questions for a work-card, teachers should try to fulfil three objectives. In the first place, pupils should be asked to find information for themselves. Secondly, an attempt might be made to encourage them to make deductions from this information; and thirdly, they might be asked to sketch or draw objects relevant to their study. These questions, for instance, would satisfy the requirements:

1. Make a list of tools and weapons used by Bronze Age men.
2. Find evidence that Iron Age men fought, grew corn, wove and had horses and carts.
3. Draw three objects which were found by archaeologists at the Roman villa of . . . . Explain the purposes of these objects.

In devising work-sheets one begins with the assumption that the most effective and most interesting means of learning is by collecting information and assessing it oneself. If children can be encouraged to read, observe and deduce, with the teacher in the rôle of a director of studies rather than as a dispenser of information, history can be said to be playing an important part in training children's minds, apart from its value of giving them some insight into the past.

A work-sheet is a term used to describe sheets of paper with headings or questions under which children write down their observations. A folder of these sheets might contain:

A plan or map of the museum, showing the route to be taken by pupils and the various rooms where exhibits are shown. The museum will usually be able to provide this plan.

A question and answer sheet which asks children to look for clues.

Blank sheets with headings under which children draw and write notes. For instance, they might have to find and draw a domestic utensil, write notes on its use and state the materials from which it was made. The work-books issued by the Geffrye Museum and the City of Liverpool Museum are produced in this form.

A sheet with a drawing already printed. The children label the parts and write notes about the exhibit.

On work-sheets one should leave space for children's answers. Specific tasks should be set, not general ones. For instance, a question might ask children to draw and list Bronze Age weapons, not all the weapons of all ages shown in the rooms. Children can be set to work in groups or as individuals, and in different rooms, so that one display case is not overcrowded. The teacher should remain in a central position to give advice. Curators can tell hair-raising stories of teachers who drop their classes on a museum for an hour while they slip away to do their shopping.

When children are studying a particular type of exhibit, it should be set in its historical context. For instance, if the children are working on medieval armour and weapons, there should be questions or discussion later on the causes and nature of medieval warfare. Similarly, if children are studying aspects of social history – furniture, dress, trades and crafts – their inquiries should be directed not only at finding out the details of these objects, but also at discovering something of the people who used them and the lives that these people led. In constructing and using work-sheets, the teacher ought to aim at this personal exploration and discovery, explanation and illustration, and the child's work should then reveal his or her personal view of what he or she has seen and to what extent the work has been understood.

Classroom completion

To gain the maximum advantage from a museum, the visit should be part of a general scheme of work or project. Whatever the plan, children can be given specific tasks in the classroom which can be developed on the visit. The information gleaned from the tour of the museum might be incorporated in a class scrapbook or in individual projects under investigation by the pupils. For instance, background books on the topics illustrated in the museum – furniture, pottery, armour – might be displayed and used. The visit can also provide inspiration for model-making, class plays and stories. General accounts on the lines of 'My Visit to the Museum' invite dull recapitulations and are to be avoided. Simply answering questions and drawing pieces of furniture can become boring too, so the wise teacher will have other aids – plasticine, paints, balsa wood and polystyrene for models, and fabrics for collages. In this way art and craft work can be integrated with history: the enthusiasm and enjoyment of children learning by doing are the teacher's reward.

Museum services

Most museum staffs welcome teachers and their pupils. However, the services provided vary in quality and must be explored personally. A list of institutions which issue catalogues, printed guides or illustrations has already been published by the Historical Association in *Guide to Illustrative Material for Use in Teaching History*, 1962. There is a list of museums which have guidebooks, postcards and illustrations for sale in *Handbook for History Teachers*, Methuen, 1962, pp. 64-5. There are omissions in these lists and museums are constantly revising their pamphlets, guides and illustrations for sale to the public, so again a personal visit or letter is to be recommended.

Some of the specialised services offered by museums follow.

Loans

Many museums have loan collections for use in schools. The National Museum of Wales at Cardiff sends out a lecturer with the exhibits, but most museums leave the teachers to use the exhibits as they wish. Loans are normally for a few days and the schools make their own transport arrangements, but a few museums handle their own distribution and collection. The exhibits on loan are often models – of a Tudor house, a local archaeological site which has been excavated, a medieval castle and so on – or a collection of objects representative of an age, like Iron Age utensils and weapons. The value of the loans is that objects can be handled and used as models for children's work. Another form of loan service is the provision of slides, filmstrips and picture collections; this can be extremely useful, especially if they are copies of old prints, engravings and photographs.

Publications

Publications can be used as sources of information, pictures and contemporary accounts. The teacher can easily create for himself a wide range of classroom material by writing a note or two on a post-card, with questions for children to answer. The following pages give some idea of the range of services offered by a number of museums. This list represents only a selection, but it does indicate the readiness of museum staffs to make their collections attractive to schoolchildren. If more teachers are tempted to sample these activities one feels that the quality of history teaching in primary and secondary schools will be vastly improved.

The City of Liverpool Museum, William Brown Street, Liverpool.

1. Study sessions are given for primary and secondary schools, sixth forms, colleges of education, WEA classes and university students. The lectures and talks are illustrated by slides or films and pupils are allowed to handle the exhibits. Practical work in the rooms follows the talks.
2. The Museum has a wide selection of workbooks which pupils complete with sketches and notes, filling in gaps in accounts, completing designs and adding some original work and ideas of their own. Some of the titles of these workbooks are: Liverpool Pottery; Treasures of the World; Ships; the Age of Victoria; Early Man; Civilisations of the Past; Look at Liverpool.
3. Two annual schools' competitions based on a Museum visit are offered. Project books, field-notes, collections, wall or table displays, friezes, murals, paintings or sets of completed workbooks can be entered.
4. Vacation courses, holiday filmshows and a holiday 'quiz' are arranged for children.
5. There is a Junior Discovery Club which meets on Saturday mornings, and the Museum

has publications, filmstrips, slides and post-cards for sale.

To provide teachers with some ideas on questions suitable for children, three examples are given below. Without the actual objects in front of us, it is not easy to appreciate the intention behind the questions, but one can see that to answer them children have to study the exhibits carefully. Educational programmes at the Museum have been deliberately designed to involve children in the Museum's activities through explanation, appreciation, handling objects and thinking about them. In many ways this Museum's services are a model of its type.

(a) 'The Victorian love for making something decorative "out of nothing" is shown in the sentimental objects and ornaments often made by the Victorian lady herself. Draw an example and state what materials were used.'
(b) (An unfinished picture of a fire engine is given.) 'Draw in the following missing parts: the brake handles, boiler, funnel, coal box, and finish the wheels.'
(c) (A caption to a steam-pump.) 'This steam-pump, built in . . . . was drawn by h . . . . . The steam engine only worked the pump which could raise steam in . . . . minutes and could force out . . . . gallons per minute. Liverpool Public Fire Service started in 18 . .; before that engines were run by I . . . . Companies.'
(d) (Drawings of ships.) 'Draw the stern of the Cinque Ports ship to show steering oar and aftercastle.'

The London Museum, Kensington Palace, London, W.8.

The London Museum employs a Schools' Officer who arranges lessons in the Museum for children of 8 to 15. Opportunities are provided for pupils to handle objects and the lessons range from prehistoric times to Victorian London. The Museum has an extensive list of postcards and pamphlets for sale. For instance, a booklet on the drawings of Thomas Rowlandson, with 24 plates, provides a vivid picture of the social scene in London between 1785 and 1820 – a very useful source of illustrations for children's work. The Museum also has a comprehensive book list for teachers, another of books suitable for children, suggestions for visits, and filmstrips for hire. Another feature of this Museum's services is a series of questionnaires linked to the contents of each room – Roman, medieval,

Tudor, Georgian and Victorian London. These sheets ask children to search for information, explain and add their comments, and to illustrate their answers. An extract from one of the question sheets is given on page 65.

Glasgow Museum, Kelvingrove, Glasgow, C.3.

A Schools' Museum Service provides the following assistance:
1. Lessons and courses, illustrated by Museum objects, charts, slides and films. Children are asked to make notes or drawings in the course of the work. Some of the subjects offered are: Early Man; Medieval Armour and Weapons; Sea Transport; the Industrial Revolution.
2. The Museum staff are ready to link up with children working on projects, either by directing them to and talking about relevant exhibits or by a lesson.
3. Film programmes – e.g. 'World War II'.

The City Museum, Queen's Road, Bristol, 8.

The Schools' Museum Service, which operates through three city museums, is staffed by trained, resident organisers who arrange a comprehensive programme for schoolchildren.

1. Loans: A catalogue is distributed to schools. Objects which may be borrowed include: specimens of flint tools; models of an Iron Age village, a Roman hypocaust and villa, an Elizabethan house, castles, churches, costume and ships; coins; armour; flintlock pistols and pottery.
2. Competitions: The Museum arranges competitions which are open to children under 16. The ideas put forward in the competitions could easily be adapted for the classroom.
3. Lessons: Organisers give lessons on subjects such as: Farming in the 19th century (based on farming tools and kitchen implements from the collection); Medieval Bristol (illustrated with maps, slides and objects); and Everyday Life in Roman Britain.
4. Children's Work: Children visiting the City Museum can use a specially equipped room, with tables, chairs, blackboard, microscope, display boards, screen, film projector and other audio-visual aids. There is a Saturday Club for children of 9 to 12 years. Displays, films and filmstrips are shown, and excursions are arranged.

The Geffrye Museum, Kingsland Road, London, E.2.

This Museum provides talks, tours, question-naires and study-notebooks. One of the outstanding features of its imaginative and thorough service is a series of printed pamphlets on Furniture, Tableware, Kitchenware, etc. For children's use the Museum publishes *Outline* books (on Costume, Streets, Transport, etc.); *English Homes*, from the 16th century to the 20th century; and a series called *Children at Home*, again from the 16th to the 20th century.

References
Barrand J., *Museums and the Teaching of History, Teaching History*, Vol. 1, No. 2, 1969
Harrison M., *Learning out of School: A Brief Guide to the Educational Use of Museums*, ESA, 1954
Harrison M., *Changing Museums: their Use and Misuse*, Longmans, 1967
Museums and Galleries in Great Britain and Northern Ireland, Index Publishers Ltd, annually
Palmer J., *Going to Museums*, Phoenix House
UNESCO, *Museums and Young People*
Winstanley B., *School-Loan Services*, Museums Association, 1959
Winstanley B., *Children and Museums*, Blackwell, 1967

The Group for Educational Services in Museums

Museum School Services

England (except London)
The American Museum, Claverton Manor, Bath.
Art Gallery Centre, 81 Princess Street, Manchester 1.
Bowes Museum, Barnard Castle, County Durham.
The Castle Museum, Norwich.
The City Museum and Art Gallery, Congreve Street, Birmingham 3.
The City Art Gallery and Museum, Cartwright Memorial Hall, Bradford 9.
The City Museum, Queen's Road, Bristol 8.
The City of Liverpool Museum, William Brown Street, Liverpool 3.
The City Museum and Art Gallery, Tavistock Road, Plymouth.
City Museum, Weston Park, Sheffield 10.
City-County Museum Service, Fletcher's House, Woodstock, Oxon.
Colchester and Essex Museum, The Castle, Colchester.

The County Museum, Church Street, Aylesbury.

The County Museum, Taunton, Somerset.

The County Museum, Market Place, Warwick.

Cross Corners, Thurcaston Road, Belgrave, Leicester.

Derbyshire Museum Service, Park Grange, Duffield Road, Derby.

Devonshire County Council Natural History Museum, Torwood Street, Torquay, Devon.

Dorman Memorial Museum, Middlesbrough, Yorkshire.

Graves Art Gallery, Surrey Street, Sheffield.

Hartlebury Castle, Kidderminster Worcestershire.

Haslemere Educational Museum, High Street, Haslemere, Surrey.

Manchester Museum, The University, Oxford Road, Manchester 13.

The Museum, St. Albans, Herts.

Municipal Buildings, Calverley Street, Leeds.

Museum and Art Gallery, Broadway, Letchworth, Herts.

Museum and Art Gallery, Wardown Park, Luton, Beds.

The Museum and Art Gallery, 28 Castle Street, Reading.

The Natural History Museum, Woolaton Hall, Nottingham.

Schools Museum Service, Westfield House, Western Road, Lewes, Sussex.

Schools Museum Service, 58 Chepstow Road, Newport, Mon.

School Service Department, The Central Library, Guildhall Square, Portsmouth.

West Riding Schools Museum Service, 71c Northgate, Wakefield, Yorks.

London

The British Museum, Bloomsbury, London, W.C.1.

The Commonwealth Institute, Kensington High Street, London, W.8.

The Geffrye Museum, Kingsland Road, London, E.2.

Horniman Museum, Forest Hill, London S.E.23.

The London Museum, Kensington Palace, Kensington Gardens, London, W.8.

The National Gallery, Trafalgar Square, London, W.C.2.

The National Maritime Museum, Greenwich, London, S.E.10.

The Science Museum, South Kensington, London, S.W.7.

The Tate Gallery, Millbank, London, S.W.1.

The Victoria and Albert Museum, Cromwell Road, South Kensington, London, S.W.7.

Scotland

The Schools Museum Service, City of Edinburgh Education Department, 12 St. Giles' Street, Edinburgh.

The Museum and Art Gallery, Kelvingrove, Glasgow, C.3.

Wales

The National Museum of Wales, Cathays Park, Cardiff.

For the addresses and brief descriptions of local and national museums, one should consult *Museums and Galleries in Great Britain and Northern Ireland*, Index Publishers, 69 Victoria Street, London, S.W.1 and *Guide to London Museums and Galleries*, HMSO.

Three work-sheets are added to indicate three different approaches to children's work in museums. The work-sheets are from:

1. The Geffrye Museum, E.2.
2. The London Museum, W.8.
3. The City Museum, Bristol.

Fill in these spaces ...then you will have a picture summary of the Museum

	16th Century	17th Century	18th Century	19th Century	20th Century
THESE MEN OR WOMEN					Man-made fabrics such as N——, R——, P—— and G—— are labour-saving, durable, colourful and often uncrushable
USED THESE CHAIRS					In the past chairs were made of o——, b——, w——, and m——, Modern chairs are also made of m—— and various kinds of p——
IN THIS PERIOD	E.................	S.................	G.................	V.................	

Worksheet. Geffrye Museum

64

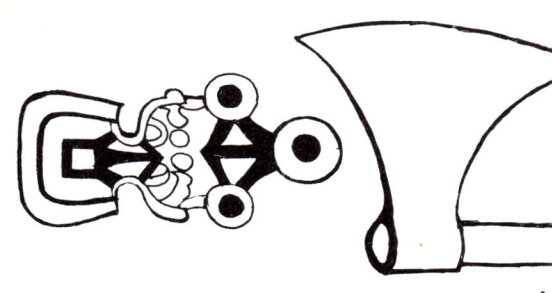

This .... belonged to a Saxon woman in the ...... century. Other objects found in graves were ......

VIKING This ...... was used by Vikings who attacked from Scandinavia in the .... century.
Sketch another object used by the Vikings from the display on the right. Use the other side of the paper.

In which centuries was Old St. Paul's built?..............

Sketch 2 kinds of windows.

London Bridge looked like this in the year........ Can you see the traitors' heads?

This jug was used in the ...... century when London was called ......

The Latin means ......

On the map –
1. Shade the Thames lightly.
2. Draw the bridge where road leads to it.
3. Name 4 gates marked.
4. Draw a circle where St. Paul's is now.

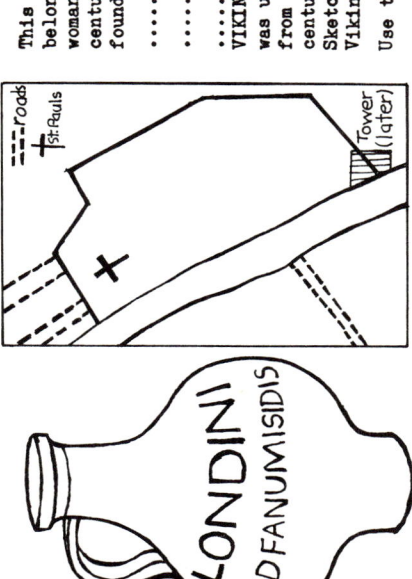

Sketch and name the arms of one guild.

List 3 others
1...............
2...............
3...............

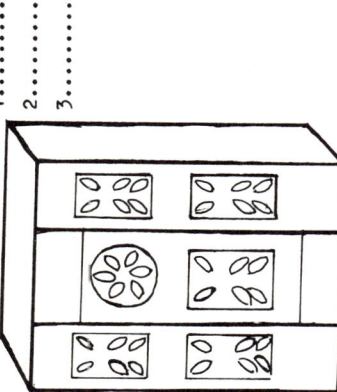

Sketch a shoe 14" long here

This .... was made in the .... century at the end of the Middle Ages.

List 2 other household objects
1...............
2...............

On the other side sketch a weapon and something for a horseman.

Look for pilgrim badges.

Name two towns visited by pilgrims.
....
....

TRANSPORT GALLERY (On first floor)

1. Magnet Coach:

This is a large coach which travelled regularly, during the last century, from London to Bushy Park and Hampton Court. It was pulled by four horses (four-in-hand).

(i) How many people could have fitted into this coach (read label)? ....

....

(ii) What do we use today instead of coaches? ....

....

Draw one of the coach lamps in this space

2. Look at the coach labelled 'Four-in-hand' (which is four coaches away).

What route did it travel? ....

3. Ambulance:

Ambulances like this one were used at the end of the 19th century.

In what way is this one different from present-day ambulances? ....

....

4. Farm Wagon:

These were common on Gloucestershire farms until fairly recently.

Why do you think it has such wide wheels (read label)? ....

....

5. Gipsy Caravan:

This caravan is one of the five types used by gipsies.

What is a gipsy? ....

Look inside the caravan, and write down 4 things which you can see inside .....

....

....

Worksheet. City Museum, Bristol

Chapter Seven   Field Studies

In the last thirty years the geographers in schools have really gripped the bit between their teeth as far as field studies are concerned and have revitalised their subject by exploring and analysing local evidence. Unfortunately, historians have dragged their feet: one indication of this has been the concentration upon geography in courses at Field Centres organised by the Council for Field Studies and other groups. And yet, when one looks at the evidence on the ground, it is apparent that the history teacher is missing important opportunities to enliven his subject. In the first place, historical remains can illustrate aspects of local history that cannot be traced in books. Again, the evidence of earth, stones and wood can very often augment the information culled from books. The greatest attraction of field studies is that they can be a practical activity, closely linked with first-hand, tangible evidence. Every parish and town has part of its history on the ground, in its Roman remains, fields, houses, public buildings, furnishings and ruins, a fact which teachers take too often for granted and in so doing miss a valuable source of historical evidence. Because of the historian's concentration on books, there is a great danger that he will lose touch with field studies and thereby lose a valuable means of awakening the curiosity of children. A. L. Rowse, in the *Use of History*, wrote that: 'The things we see around us, town or village, a church, a harbour or bit of wall, even a field or stretch of landscape, are all documents for history as much as a charter or a land-book, a title-deed, a letter or a will. Very often the two relate to each other. . . . They illuminate each other'.

The investigation of field remains can be used to illustrate past societies, and it is possible to ask children to make deductions from evidence about the lives of the people who lived there. If the field visit is linked to a museum visit, other evidence can be used – inscriptions, coins, furniture, domestic utensils and weapons.

Many schools throughout the country have developed practical and imaginative schemes based on local field studies, but many teachers are uncertain of how to go about directing fieldwork. The various practical schemes outlined in *Field Studies for Schools* edited by M. S. Dilke, will do much to hearten and encourage those who contemplate such work, and this chapter seeks to prepare the teacher for practical activities linked to field visits.

Types of field study

There are several different categories of historical field studies that might be attempted by schoolchildren. One form of study is linked to local history. By using maps and documentary evidence such as charters, turnpike and enclosure awards, children can explore the evidence on the ground, noting the alterations to the landscape affected by the changes in agriculture and roads.[1] This form of investigation normally takes the shape of a topic, for complete historical surveys are beyond the resources and capabilities of schoolchildren. Some of the topics that have been tackled successfully include agriculture, transport and communications, industry, settlements, architecture, place-names and town development. Another approach is to examine individual sites within the county. One wishes that more colleges of education or teachers' associations would

[1] One example of this type of work is reported on in *Approaches to Fieldwork in History in the Primary School*, in *Teaching History*, Vol. 1, No. 3, 1970.

follow the example of a group of County Durham schoolteachers and lecturers who have published *History Field Studies in the Durham Area.* (University of Durham Institute of Education, 1966), which gives details – both historical and geographical – of more than thirty sites which can be visited by children.

Archaeological sites

Some local remains might serve as an introduction to archaeology, which is no longer restricted to the study of prehistoric or Roman remains, as it once was. Since 1945 the study of medieval archaeology and the investigation of 18th and 19th century industrial sites have become extremely popular, even fashionable. Indeed, if one thinks of archaeology from the school viewpoint, it is in this latter field that children can be more actively involved. One may be fortunate in having on the staff a classical scholar who is willing to surrender his weekends for the History Society or who can offer his contribution to a General Studies course by excavating a local site. Such men are rare.

Teachers who have had little training or experience in archaeological work ought not to attempt any excavation without expert assistance. Many valuable sites have been irreparably damaged by gangs of enthusiastic but clumsy youngsters. Archaeology is a complex and scientific technique and should be left to those with specialist knowledge. If children and their teachers are willing to join an excavation team to learn the skills under the guidance of a qualified archaeologist, the local librarian or historical society will be able to give details of excavations planned or in progress. The extra-mural departments of the universities and local archaeological societies are the major mentors in this business.

Yet, archaeological sites do have an important rôle to play in teaching history. Children can gain valuable insight into prehistoric societies by visiting hill-forts, barrows and camps. Here is an opportunity to use the vivid imaginations that children possess. A hill-fort might look, to an unpractised eye, like any other field or stretch of moorland. But children can be set tasks on the ground: measuring the bounds of the fort by tape-measure or paces; making sketches of the main features of the fortifications; guessing at the entrances and defence works – ditches, banks and mounds – by walking carefully over the ground. Then, in the classroom, comes the follow-up – paintings of the fort, the study of an air photograph and an article (if one exists) in

the *Proceedings* of the archaeological society; the construction of plans from measurements taken on the site; accounts of other Iron-Age forts. In this respect the local museum is often valuable not only because it has on display objects found in the fort, but also because the staff may be able to lend the school flints, weapons and domestic articles which they have been able to duplicate in the museum.

The landscape

Another feature of local field studies might well be an investigation of the landscape. To begin with the teacher might take his pupils around the boundaries of the ancient parish (if it is a village school) or the old town (from an urban school). The route can be traced from photocopies of old maps of the parish. The civil parish, which is marked on Ordnance Survey maps, may or may not coincide with the boundaries of the ancient ecclesiastical parish. Many civil parish bounds are the consequence of 19th century administrative changes. The boundaries of the older parish can often be obtained from a tithe map. All historical features of interest should be noted by children in their books as they walk around the parish or town, and perhaps the camera can record interesting remains. Ditches, boundary walls, banks, woods, roads, unusual buildings, lanes and old shops can be noted. Valuable advice on these topics is given in *Field Studies: Some Notes for Beginners* (HMSO).

It is not difficult to take the text of a local charter and identify boundary points, either on the six-inch OS map or on the ground, although as Professor Hoskins points out, 'the alder tree or the broken stump' will have long since disappeared. If the school is fortunate enough to have Roman remains, a known deserted village or a moated homestead site within easy reach, there are obviously many more opportunities for practical work. The HMSO map of Roman Britain is a useful guide. For deserted villages, M. W. Beresford in *The Lost Villages of England* has some suggestions. Of course, digging should not be attempted without expert assistance, but children can still be asked to sketch, measure and draw without fear of damage to the site. If some excavation has taken place, the local museum will doubtless have shards of pottery, photographs and other details.

It is possible to take a local topic, examine the evidence on the ground, and then enlarge upon it. The Industrial Revolution is a case in point: the evidence of industrial changes in Birmingham, Manchester or other towns and cities can provide a valuable insight into national problems of poverty, housing, sanitation, transport and technology introduced by changes in industrial techniques in the 18th and 19th centuries.

Some schools organise visits lasting a week to places of historical interest – York, Chester, Hadrian's Wall, London, Gloucester – to give children an insight into evidence on the ground far removed from their own locality. These excursions, needless to say, require careful preparation and the best results are achieved if children are required to keep log-books, answer questionnaires, sketch architectural details and record information in various ways.

Villages and towns

Villages and towns are more suited to field study than archaeological sites simply because there is more observable evidence. The questions that a teacher can ask about villages might deal with the choice of site (soil, water supply, relief, communications); the location of early buildings (manor house, church, watermill); the evidence of later building; enclosure and the results of industrialisation. Maps and fieldwork can reveal links with market towns, turnpike routes, milestones, signposts, railway or canal buildings, open fields and relics of older village industries – the smithy, mills, quarries and kilns.

With towns, the problem is much greater, and it may be best to concentrate on a topic – like industrialisation – or an area. Using maps, children can be asked to spot the market place, public buildings, fortifications and the sites of early industries. Towns largely develop because of their communications and there is usually ample evidence of roads, canals and railways. Maps, sale catalogues, newspaper advertisements and directories provide much material for studying the physical growth of towns, but a survey of streets can be useful in spotting architectural details, inn signs and street names.

Industrial archaeology

Prehistoric and Roman remains such as forts, villas, urban dwellings and defence works have normally been studied in detail. The same might be said of medieval castles and larger ecclesiastical buildings, but not of moated homesteads, mottes, tumuli and the remains of deserted villages, all of which appear on large scale Ordnance Survey maps but may not have been excavated or described. These mottes and mounds can provide children with valuable

field work and experience. By producing written and illustrated descriptions, measured drawings and photographs, children can not only learn something of these remains but perhaps add to local knowledge.

Industrial archaeology offers possibly the greatest opportunity for children's work at this level. The evidence of industrial activity ranges over a number of centuries, but it is the buildings and machinery of the industrial revolution of the 18th and 19th centuries – turnpike roads, enclosure, canals, bridges, disused railways, coaching inns, factories and mills – which afford the teacher the opportunity to investigate remains at first hand.

Visits to buildings

The objectives, methods and consequences of taking children into buildings under public and private ownership should bear the same rigorous scrutiny that accompanies other educational schemes mentioned in this book. One takes children to Fountains Abbey, Cardiff Castle and St. Albans for them to see, observe and record and by these activities learn something of monastic, military and Roman life. Children have keen eyes and keen imaginations but, not surprisingly, they are untrained observers. Therefore, a jaunt around a castle or a museum will have some educational value but how much will depend on the extent of children's work associated with the visit. Assuming that one is taking a class of thirty children to a historical building, there are various options open to the teacher in organising the visit.

1. A conducted tour with the teacher, guide book in hand, as the leader.
2. A conducted tour with a resident or official as the guide.
3. A free-wheeling visit, with children let loose with thirty guide books, to find their own way around.
4. A brief introductory talk from a vantage point by the curator or teacher, followed by the distribution of work-sheets to individuals and groups.

Although 1 and 2 are the more usual methods of organising a visit, 4 has considerable educational value. However, some houses have fixed tours and fixed routes where children cannot wander at will. Some teachers might be reluctant, thinking of the children, parents and the law-courts, to allow pupils to clamber over ruined keeps or gape down to the Wye from the battlements of Chepstow Castle. Even if one plays safe and employs the second method, work-sheets can still be issued so that some discovery and deduction are possible by the pupils. The objectives are clear: we want children to relate the information in the guide book to the evidence before their eyes, to use their imaginations and to understand something of the lives of the people who lived there. To some extent this can be done by means of a conducted tour, but a great deal more excitement and real learning can be generated if thirty guide books are distributed and children are encouraged to observe, record and analyse for themselves.

The history of buildings is a special topic in itself. In the classroom it widens out to the study of settlement and the distribution of buildings for particular reasons. Geography, history and architecture are involved, and the subject lends itself to fieldwork, illustration and analysis. For instance, children can be set quite detailed investigations into land utilisation, architectural styles, the use of local materials and the classification of buildings by function. Buildings are useful as starting points for local studies. Why were these sites chosen? Who were the first occupiers? How was the supply of food and water guarded? What were the means of defence, of communication and supply? Why did this house or castle decay and the other survive? What reasons lie behind the shape and size of this village: is it a main road, a river crossing, good farming land, or a good defensive position? These are the sort of questions that children can answer, given the opportunity to consult books and to roam around a habitation.

When working out a scheme for a visit, one should bear in mind that the general setting of the building should be studied first. The reasons for a choice of site, the natural features, the name and its significance, the ground and the out-buildings: all these points bear consideration. One can then move on to the main construction: why and when was it erected? Does the building still serve its original purpose? If not, in what ways has it been altered to suit changing circumstances? Are there any blocked windows or doors, additional defensive features, later decorative or utilitarian additions? Were the materials – stone, tile, wood, flint, brick, thatch – obtained locally?

Inside the building, the same critical approach can be followed. How many floors are there? What were the purposes of the different rooms? Here the sketch book should come out. Sketches of chimneys, windows, doors, staircases, cellars and battlements should be made. Similarly, children can be asked to answer questions and make sketches of furniture, armour, paintings and portraits if the house has collections of these items.

In this way cathedrals, abbeys and monasteries, parish churches, castles, country houses and town buildings will be looked at critically, a training which the child might well carry through his adult life. The difference between this form of directed learning and the conducted tour is the difference between a critical appraisal and un-informed gawping.

Individual buildings

Churches: Children might begin by surveying the surroundings of the church – almshouses, gateway, gravestones, the parsonage – together with the materials used in the construction. Then, by sketching and adding notes, each part of the church can be examined in turn – porch, door, font, nave, aisles, screen, side chapels, chancel arch and altar. The fittings in the church often provide valuable sources – piscina, pulpit, lectern, sedilia, stone memorials, brasses, poor box, pews, stained glass windows and the tower and its bells.

Castles: One very popular topic in schools is castles, a subject also suitable for fieldwork. To begin with, one should have a reasonable collection of books on castles in the classroom, including six or more copies of the guide book to the castle to be visited. Groups of pupils or individuals can be asked to master the details of different aspects of castles – the keep, dungeons, walls, barbican, sallyport, garderobes, hall, and so on. They can then be asked to explain the details of these features to the other children on the site or to present a written report with photographs and notes on their speciality. During the visit the teacher should provide some opportunity for children to discover and record items of information for themselves and to make sketches or diagrams. This sort of visit links up well with the photo-play techniques mentioned in chapter 8.

Children's work

The age range of children has to be carefully considered in any scheme of field work. For juniors, between the ages of nine and eleven, an exploration is an exciting occasion and, for practical purposes, it is better to concentrate on local studies, although some schools do take children to another part of the country for a field week. The local environment known but not understood has greatest impact, however.

The teacher might begin by taking pupils on carefully planned walks through the town or into the countryside, pointing out specific points of importance, stopping to sketch or make notes, and linking up with earlier class discussions. Back in the classroom, children are normally very keen to follow this work up by bringing photographs from home and by constructing a scrapbook or another form of record of what they have seen. Edward Osmond, in *A Valley Grows Up*, has shown the exciting possibilities of work at this level.

This approach can also be attempted with secondary pupils, but the work can be more varied and more systematic and ought to allow these pupils to carry out appraisals of the significance of the evidence. Subjects such as housing, communications, local industry and local government can be analysed more effectively. Older children can progress to individual studies and can be set tougher assignments on field courses and on visits.

With pupils who are approaching the end of their school careers, local studies and fieldwork can be linked to the outside world. Professor W. A. L. Blyth, in *Field Studies for Schools*, mentions a study made by senior pupils of the impact on a local town of a recession in the cotton industry. From the evidence they collected the pupils went on to discuss the reasons for the depression and the schemes to assist the unemployed. This analysis of a real social problem is much more effective in training responsible citizens than classroom lessons on civics.

In all types of school one would like to see teachers using questionnaires or work-sheets more effectively. Instead of providing pupils with information, one should try as far as possible to allow children to discover for themselves. Where was the earliest inhabited place? Who chose it? Why? How were food, water, defence and shelter provided for? Is there any evidence of a well, a spring, river, ford or bridge? Why did this settlement grow? Why does this village or town have this particular shape?

Whatever the age or ability group, fieldwork has to be carefully organised with thorough preparation by the teacher before the class moves outside school. The classroom introduction might be achieved by reading, by consulting maps and aerial photographs and by making notes. One method of involving children deeply in the actual visit is to warn them that during the excursion each pupil or group has to make notes on a specific aspect of the building or site that is to be examined. This direct participation can be most effective, for on the return to the classroom each group can continue working on the material collected in the field and then report to the rest of the class on the results of their particular survey. The completed work might be presented as a scrapbook, a booklet or an oral report to the rest of the class.

Fieldwork is not easy. It requires careful preparation in class; liaison with public libraries to obtain books for preliminary and follow-up work by teachers and children; detailed administration with bus companies, curators, guides and headmasters; and a readiness to cope with the emergencies that inevitably arise. However, once these arrangements have been made, fieldwork can become an immensely rewarding activity. Children at last come into touch with real places and things and, in a bookish subject such as history, this is always to be welcomed, especially for less able children. By looking closely at a building one's pupils can understand something of the difficulties of working and living in past societies. The offensive and defensive strategies of the Roman army take on a new meaning for children who have examined a fort, camp or road at first hand. Through field studies one hopes that children will come to appreciate the richness of the historical legacy around them and at the same time share in an imaginative experience. Perhaps they will miss this excitement, for one reason or another, but it will not be for lack of effort by the teacher.

Some schemes of work

There is space to give only one or two examples of fieldwork that might be attempted by school-children. One very popular topic in schools is the history of castles, a subject suitable for field studies. Every castle is worthy of investigation and it is not difficult, given a reconnaissance visit and a number of guide books for class use, to devise schemes for children. There are some general questions that would cover a great many castles, and if the features referred to here are not contained in the particular castle one has in mind, adaptation is a simple operation.

Again, one works from the assumption that it is better to guide children to the sources of

An eighteenth century charcoal blast furnace
By courtesy of the Science Museum

information than to spoon-feed them. Secondly, one aims to make children think about the problems of living in a castle and the tactics of attack and defence. Lastly, one aims at the 'imaginative experience' that might come from sketching, painting, recording and imagining the everyday details of life in a stone fortress. Questions that might be asked along these lines could include the following:

1. What are the advantages of this castle's site?
2. Who built the castle? When? Was it ever attacked and captured?
3. If there is a barbican and gatehouse, sketch them as they might have appeared when the castle was in use. Find the portcullis, draw-bridge and any machicolations.
4. Can you find any arrow slits, holes for pouring boiling water over attackers, grooves for the portcullis, a ditch or a moat?
5. How thick are the curtain walls? Are there any embrasures, merlons and crenellations? Sketch these parts of the battlements.
6. What do you think are the weaknesses of this castle?
7. Why were towers built on the walls? How many are there?
8. What is the purpose of the ward or bailey?
9. Find the well or other form of water supply for the castle.
10. Take up a position on the battlements. Describe the chief features of the surrounding countryside. Imagine you are the attacking commander. What orders would you give to try to force an entry?
11. Find the postern gate, an oubliette and a dungeon. What were their uses?

The variation of questions (and answers) is, of course, endless. In the classroom later children can write up their answers, illustrating them wherever possible by paintings and sketches. From the evidence the children have gathered it is not difficult to proceed to an examination of the various stages in the development of castles, working from library and class books. Taking this a stage further, an extract from a typical questionnaire based on a visit to Chepstow Castle is added, together with a photograph of the main Gatehouse to give point to the questions.

Chepstow Castle

Gatehouse and Marten's Tower

1. Look closely at the main Gatehouse. Write down six features of the entrance that would assist the defenders of the castle (cliff, round towers, portcullises, doors, arrow slit windows, machicolations, etc.).
2. Find the grooves for the portcullises. How was the portcullis raised and lowered?
3. How many storeys and how many rooms were there in the Gatehouse? What was each room used for?
4. What materials have been used in the construction of the Gatehouse?

Marten's Tower

5. Why is 'Marten's Tower' so called?
6. Have the outside walls of the Tower been strengthened?
7. Make a sketch of the Tower, labelling its most distinctive features.
8. The Tower contains a chapel and a solar. Find them. Sketch one of the architectural details – the lancet window, a fireplace, or the east window of the chapel or the battlements.

In the classroom

9. Suppose you were attacking the castle. Explain which you think is its weakest part, and with sketches and diagrams describe how an assault could be made.
10. Paint or draw a picture of the castle as it might have looked in 1403 when it was defended by the Duke of Norfolk and a garrison against the forces of the Welsh rebel, Owen Glendower.

Enclosure

The eighteenth century enclosure movement is another topic which can be taught in schools through fieldwork. However, few historical subjects can be studied in isolation in the field or anywhere else, and enclosures require a detailed study of maps, the analysis of the Award either in the record office or from a photocopied abstract of the Award used in the classroom, and work on the ground itself. By using work-sheets and maps children can in fact accomplish a piece of elementary research or at all events appreciate something of the methods that historians apply to the analysis of source material. The local museum might possess farm implements, clothing, carts and machinery which can be studied and sketched. The library might possess old maps, modern OS maps and books of a general nature on enclosures or farm practice. All these materials can be fused into a practical scheme of work.

The Enclosure Map and Award can first of all be studied in the classroom. One can obtain

Chepstow Castle
Crown copyright

Ridge and furrow in the Midlands
By courtesy of Aerofilms Ltd.

photocopies of an Award and the accompanying map at a reasonable cost from the local record office. If there is an earlier map showing the open fields – on an estate or tithe map – children can study conditions before and after an Act and an Award. If an earlier map is not available, one could use a picture, photograph or sketch of a village with the open fields displayed.

Shown on page 75 is an aerial photograph of a Midlands landscape taken in the evening when the shadows were long and the ridges and furrows can be clearly seen. Children can use this picture as a guide to the investigation of medieval farming. For instance, questions might be set as follows:

1. How many large open fields can you see in this picture? What crops would have been grown in the fields in medieval times?
2. Smaller units of cultivation called 'furlongs' were ploughed within the open fields. Can you find a furlong in this picture? What is the measurement of a furlong today?
3. What were 'common balks'? Can you find any in this picture?
4. What additions to the landscape have been made since the days of the open fields?

Fieldwork:
5. Can you find any evidence of ridge and furrow or open fields in your area? Mark these places on a map of your own making.
6. Can you find any evidence of medieval farming in your own locality – a manor house; field or road names such as Glebe Road, Woodman's Way, Lea Road and Meadow Lane; banks or ditches; common land; deserted villages and other remains? Plot these places on your map.

By using an *Enclosure Act and Award*, children can then proceed to a comparison between medieval and later methods of farming. Questions can be set on the Enclosure Map and Award as follows:

1. Who was appointed to make the Award?
2. What proportion (roughly) of the land in the parish was enclosed by this Act? Draw a sketch map, shading in the enclosed land.
3. Of the land not enclosed, was there any common land?
4. Who were the chief landowners and landholders named in the Award?
5. Were any new farms built after enclosure? Mark them on your map.
6. Were any new roads made under the Award? Add them to your map.

7. Can you find the old open fields? Draw another map to show them. Mark the church, the manor house and any other important buildings.
8. Look up the derivation of the old farm and field names.

Fieldwork:
9. Find the buildings named on the Enclosure Map – church, manor house, the larger farmhouses.
10. Take the enclosures of one major landowner shown in the Award and find out what has happened to the land since the date of the Award. Are there any new farms and new roads? What crops are now grown on the enclosed fields? Are any fields for grazing? Have the enclosed fields been subdivided by hedges or ditches? What new houses or industrial buildings have been added since the Act?

After the visit
Children should now be able to adapt their knowledge to the historical significance of enclosure: why it was necessary; the consequences throughout Britain for the landowners, farmers and labourers; and the improvements in cultivation and machinery that accompanied the revolution on the land. Children could be set work on Jethro Tull, Robert Bakewell and Arthur Young; they could be asked to summarise the advantages and disadvantages of enclosure and to find out what agrarian changes have taken place in their village in the last two hundred years. Scrapbooks on subjects such as 'Our Changing Countryside', 'The Agrarian Revolution' and 'The Village' can be compiled with maps, plans and photographs as illustrations. *The Agrarian Revolution* by John Addy in the *Then and There* series is extremely valuable for work at this level.

The Enclosure of Deerhurst, Glos., 1815
The enclosure award map for Deerhurst, Glos., a section of which is shown here, shows clearly the awards of land made to the major landowners. The Commissioners, when plotting the survey, noticed Jeremiah Hawkins of the Haw crossing the river on horseback to reach his estate on the east bank and added him to their map.

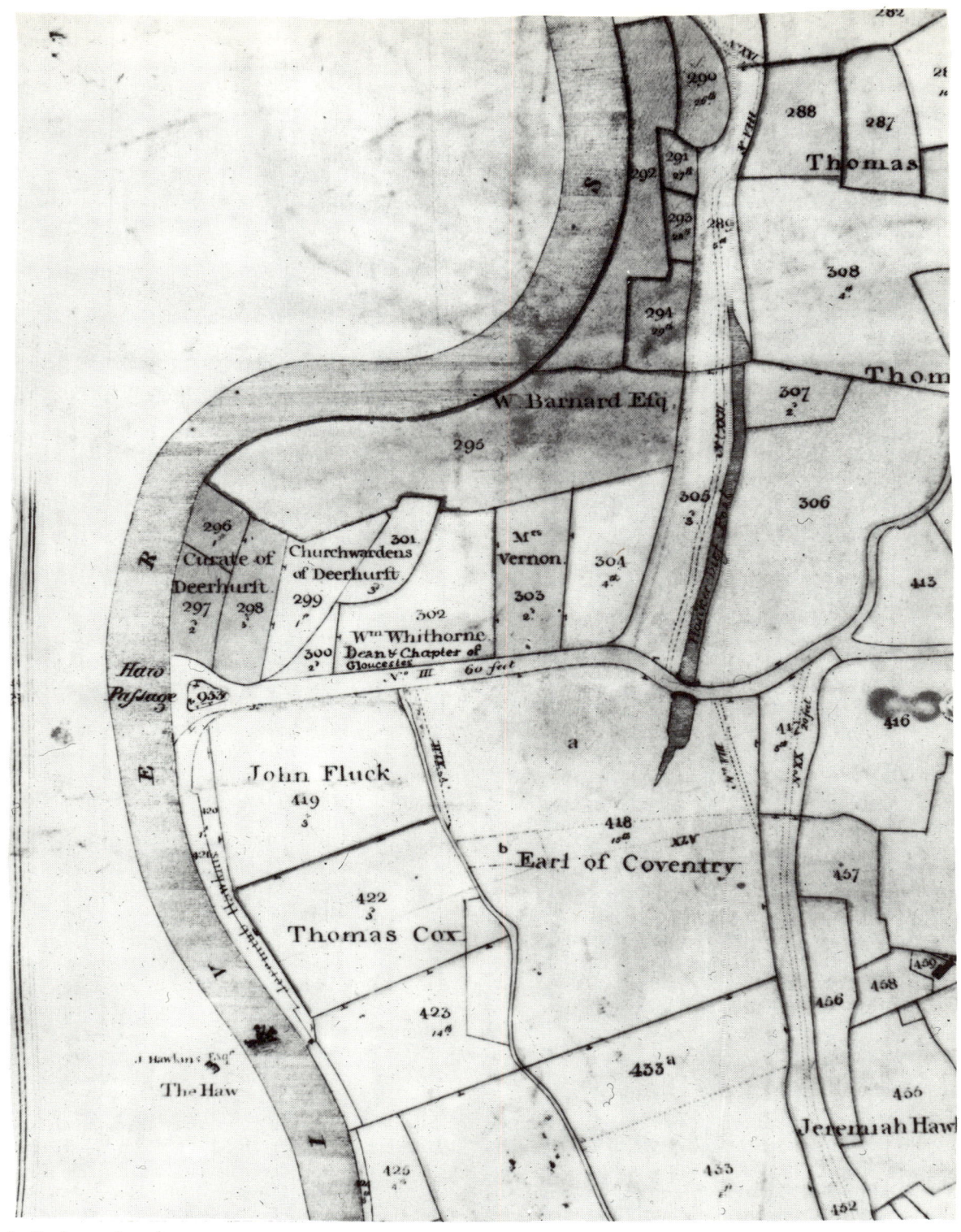

An Enclosure Award map
By courtesy of Leigh Parish Council and Gloucestershire County Council

References: 1

Some General Books on Field Studies

Bracey H. E., *Village Survey*, Methuen, 1953

Bracey H. E., *Country Town Survey*, Methuen, 1954

Council for British Archaeology, *The Investigation of Smaller Domestic Buildings*, 1959

Corfe T. (editor), *History in the Field*, Blond, 1970

Doncaster I. J., *Finding the History Around Us*, Blackwell, 1956

Doncaster I. J., *Discovering Man's Habitat*, National Froebel Foundation, 1963

Dilke M. S. (ed.), *Field Studies for Schools*, Vol. 1 The Purpose and Organization of Field Studies, Vols. 2-7 Field Excursions (2 in North-West England, 3 in Eastern Scotland, 4 in North Wales, 5 in Eastern England, 6 in West Scotland, 7 in the East Midlands), Rivingtons, 1965–70

Fellows A., *The Wayfarer's Companion*, OUP, 1937

Hadfield C., *British Canals*, Phoenix, 1959

Hadfield C. (ed.), *The Canals of the British Isles*, David and Charles

Hoskins W. G., *Local History in England*, Longmans, 1959

Hoskins W. G., *The Making of the English Landscape*, Hodder and Stoughton, 1965

Hoskins W. G., *Field Studies in Local History*, Faber, 1967

Rolt L. T. C., *Motoring History*, Vista, 1964

Schreiber H., *The History of Roads*, Barrie and Rockliff, 1961

Simmons J., *Transport*, Vista, 1962

Simmons J., *The Railways of Britain*, Routledge, 1961

Simpson C. A., *Making Local Surveys; An Eye for Country*, Pitman, 1951

Stewart C. A., *A Village Surveyed*, Arnold, 1948

Thomas St. John D. (ed.), *A Regional History of the Railways of Great Britain*, David and Charles

References: 2

Archaeology

For details of excavations in progress the teacher should consult the Council of British Archaeology, 4 St. Andrew's Place, London, N.W.1, which publishes details of regional groups and lists of forthcoming excavations. The Ministry of Public Building and Works, Lambeth Bridge House, London, S.E.1, will supply information and guide books for sites under its supervision.

For local surveys, a ready supply of local maps should be available. The Ordnance Survey or their agents will be able to supply the 2½-inch, 6-inch and 25-inch maps and these contain details of archaeological sites. Otherwise the teacher should consult local sources, or the *Sectional List No. 27; Ancient Monuments and Historic Buildings* (HMSO), which gives details of the Ministry of Works' publications.

Atkinson R. J. C., *Field Archaeology*, 2nd edition, Methuen, 1963

Beresford M. W., *History on the Ground*, Lutterworth, 1957

Beresford M. W. and St. Joseph J. K. S., *Medieval England; An Aerial Survey*, CUP, 1958

Bruce Mitford R. L. S. (ed.), *Recent Archaeological Excavations in Great Britain*, Routledge, 1956

HMSO, *Field Archaeology; Some Notes for Beginners,* 4th edition, 1963

HMSO, *The Historian's Guide to Ordnance Survey Maps,* 1965

Hudson K., *Industrial Archaeology; An Introduction*, John Baker, 1963

Hudson K., *The Industrial Archaeology of Southern England*, David and Charles, 1964

Pannell J. P. M., *The Techniques of Industrial Archaeology*, David and Charles, 1966

Piggott S., *Approach to Archaeology*, Black, 1960

Smith D., *Industrial Archaeology of the East Midlands*, David and Charles, 1965

Stewart J., *An Archaeological Guide and Glossary*, Phoenix, 1960

Webster G., *Practical Archaeology*, Black, 1963

Wood E. S., *A Field Guide to Archaeology*, Collins, 1963

References: 3

Buildings

For a list of *houses and sites* open to the public, teachers should consult:

Historic Houses, Castles and Gardens in Great Britain and Ireland, Index publishers, annually

Sectional List No. 27; Ancient Monuments and Historic Buildings, HMSO. This List gives details of the county inventories of the Royal Commission on Historical Monuments. These list earthworks, sites and monuments and are well illustrated

C. Hussey and J. Cornforth, *English Country*

Houses Open to the Public, 4th edition, Country Life, 1964; this is a useful guide

J. Lees Milne, *The National Trust Guide: Buildings*, Batsford, 1948

Anderson M. D., *Looking for History in British Churches*, Murray, 1951

Betjeman J. (ed.), *Guide to English Parish Churches*, Collins, 1958

Chaloner W. H. and Musson A. E., *Industry and Technology*, Studio Vista, 1963

Cook G. H., *English Monasteries in the Middle Ages*, Phoenix, 1961

Cook G. H., *The English Cathedral*, Phoenix, 1957

Cox J. D. and Ford C. B., *The English Parish Church*, Batsford, 1935

Davey N., *A History of Building Materials*, Phoenix, 1961

Johns E., *British Townscapes*, Arnold, 1965

Martin G., *The Town*, Studio Vista, 1961

Meeks C. L. V., *The Railway Station*, Architectural Press, 1959

Needham A., *How to Study an Old Church*, Batsford, 1948

Sharp T., *The Anatomy of a Village*, Penguin, 1946

Taylor A. C., *The Pattern of English Building*, Batsford, 1965

Vale E., *How to Look at old buildings*, Batsford, 1946

For castles and houses the following are useful:

Barley M. W., *The House and the Home*, Studio Vista, 1963

Braun H., *The English Castle*, Batsford, 1936

Brown R. A., *English Castles*, Batsford, 1962

Dutton R., *The English Country House*, Batsford, 1962

O'Neil B. St. J., *Castles*, HMSO, 1954

For local material consult:

Pevsner N., *The Buildings of England*, Penguin Books, 1951; this series gives details of buildings of all types and dates.

The *Shell Guides*, *Little Guides* and the *Victoria County History* are useful.

However, most public buildings have guide books on sale at reasonable prices and the hard-pressed teacher may well find his reading restricted to these brief but comprehensive guides.

Chapter Eight

Active History

History teaching is very largely a matter of imaginative reconstruction of past societies. Some teachers can do this skilfully by oral methods, that is, by narrative storytelling and by a bewitching use of descriptive language. Others cannot, and for them a more practical, concrete approach might be more successful. Moreover, there are many children who simply cannot follow oral teaching for very long periods. They find it difficult to absorb information and ideas in any form at any one time. They prefer to deal with particular events and specific objects rather than with abstract ideas and generalities. These children have for long been sadly neglected. The history teacher is in general too inclined to go on talking to an increasingly inattentive audience and to relegate practical methods to the art room and the workshop. Yet the great majority of children up to the age of 15-16 do not go much beyond the practical, concrete stage of learning and history teachers might be better employed in devising and directing alternative forms of teaching, that will actively involve them in the subject.

'Active' history means any method which involves children personally and more deeply in their studies. Pupils who are intently reading a book or who are recording items of information from books, using the indexes, are actively engaged. There does not need to be movement, noise or an end-product such as a model or a play for children to be active. But there are many children who will not be able to sit for long periods with a book, and for them drama, modelling, pictorial representation, the construction of group or class textbooks, visits and photography might bring to them the enjoyment of history that is too often lacking in classrooms today.

Pictorial work

There are various techniques of presenting information and ideas in pictorial form that might be attempted by children. Painting, sketching, drawing and tracing are some of the main straightforward methods. However, there are variations that one can try. Mosaics, stained glass windows and the construction of friezes and models are other valuable forms of practical work.

Mosaics

Mosaics can be made by cutting up sheets of coloured sticky paper into squares. The pieces are stuck to a strong cardboard base, on which the outline of the subject has already been drawn. A lesson on Roman villas and temples can be illustrated by constructing a mosaic. Another method is to collect tesserae – pieces of coloured tile and crockery – and to fit them together on a base of plasticine to make a brightly coloured mosaic. Pieces of eggshell can be used in this way, mounted on plasticine and then painted or coloured to represent a mosaic from a villa floor.

Collages and montages are popular with children of all ages and can be made from various types of fabric.

Friezes

One of the most popular group activities is making a frieze, that is a set of drawings with footnotes mounted along a classroom wall. A roll of plain wallpaper makes an excellent base, and the individual pictures can be pinned or glued to it. One type of frieze tells a story in a series of pictures in sequence. They are useful for a story (like the Norman Conquest) or for a biography.

Another activity is to encourage children to

Fabric collage 'The Norman soldier and his wife' produced by a girl aged 10 years. Constructed from a linen background with coloured materials stitched to it.
By courtesy of Miss Eugenie Alexander and *Art and Craft in Education*

draw frieze figures on sugar paper. The picture is coloured by filling in the figure with crepe paper soaked in paste. Hair, the face, helmets and armour can be added by sticking paper or material to the crepe when it has dried. The crepe figures are then carefully cut out and glued to the wall frieze. The dress of Roman, Saxon, Norman, Tudor and Stuart people has been demonstrated in this way. Similarly, houses and transport can be illustrated from these materials. Another method is to paste paper figures on to cardboard. The shapes are cut out, a matchbox is then attached to each of the cut-outs and the box is in turn glued to the frieze.

A frieze or collage can be made from a mounting board. Each member of the group draws, colours and cuts out card shapes, for instance of ships in the Armada. The shapes are mounted and an explanation is added below. Card panels are similar. Here each child designs and colours a panel to illustrate a theme such as the Norman Conquest. The panels are mounted in progression, or one above the other to give a totem-pole effect.

Stained glass windows

Children can make copies of stained glass while they are learning about medieval churches or simply as a means of expressing their own ideas in a different form. A window can be made from pieces of polythene. The 'lead' in the window is drawn with a black felt-tip pen and the 'glass' part is filled in with ink or felt pens of different colours. The polythene can then be mounted on a background of coloured paper. Alternatively, if one wishes to show the whole window rather than one or two panes of glass, the outline of the window is drawn on a large sheet of paper and the glass apertures are then cut out. Coloured sheets of cellophane are pasted behind the frame. If the frame can be sellotaped to the classroom window, the sunlight shining through the coloured paper gives a striking effect.

Models

History teachers are now a great deal less critical of practical activities in the classroom than they were some years ago. The aptitude that colleagues in the science and geography departments have shown in applying informal methods to school work has encouraged many history teachers to follow their example. However, one does not immediately associate laboratories, craftrooms, benches, modelling materials and tools with history teaching. History is all too often confined to the limits of the classroom and the textbook.

In the first place the history teacher ought to campaign vigorously for a History Room. A good

Models for the history class. This collection shows (from left to right):

A motte and bailey castle (cardboard and paper)
Part of a Tudor house (cardboard and paper)
Stephenson's Rocket (cardboard and paper)
Two knights (egg boxes)
A manor house

A wooden catapult
A keep and bailey (cardboard on wooden base)
Abbey church (Polystyrene)
A Viking ship (plasticine, wooden base, dowel rod)
A Tudor shop

case for such a room was argued by the History section of the I.A.A.M. in *The Teaching of History* and by F. J. Dwyer in the *Handbook for History Teachers*. Ideally, one would like to see a History Room that is a workshop, cinema, stage, library, museum, stockroom and students' centre all rolled into one. A 'converted' classroom is unlikely to provide these facilities, and the history teacher has really to begin a fight for suitable accommodation that was won long ago by the scientists and geographers, and is increasingly being won by the specialists in modern languages. However, for the teacher who cannot obtain the specialist equipment because of financial or building considerations, there are still opportunities for improvisation. Peg-board and pin-boarding are not expensive and can often be erected by the caretaker or the boys. A room that has cupboards, desks and chairs covers the basic needs. Displays of pictures, scrapbooks and paintings can be pinned to boarding or sello-taped to walls. Cartridge paper or the backs of maps can be used as a screen, and toilet paper can serve an additional purpose for tracings. Teachers will be able to think of other ways in which a room can be made into an attractive laboratory with a little ingenuity and initiative, and at a small financial outlay.

Model-making on its own has limited value. To be effective, the subject to be modelled should be covered first by reading assignments or class lessons. Once interest has been aroused, children often want to express their ideas in models or on paper, and this is the time to begin practical work. For instance, cardboard and paste models of knights, armour and weapons might follow some class lessons on medieval warfare: then the children will be more knowledgeable about their work and detail will be more accurate. Historical accuracy is important and the teacher should aim at it as far as possible. However, modelling can provide opportunities for children's ideas and skills, and one ought not to attach too much value to absolute accuracy. If one did, there would be no modelling. From experience one has found that most children value accurate work; they are harsh on inaccuracies either in their own work or that of others.

Very few teachers of history are also teachers of craft subjects, and the lack of expertise and confidence in handling even simple materials is an effective deterrent. One essential aid is the magazine *Art & Craft in Education* (monthly; Evans Brothers, Montague House, Russell Square, London, W.C.1), which very often gives valuable advice on the construction of historical models. The writers of articles in this magazine often stress the value of model-making as a children's activity. By making a model of a castle or an Elizabethan theatre, they argue, children can more easily understand some of the problems associated with architecture and building construction. Children have to make close observations of contemporary styles and materials; they become aware of the problems of living and working in these buildings and they learn something of furniture, weapons, costume and machinery. Model-making also serves as a training in craftsmanship, in keen observation and in working with varied materials. All too often model-making is consigned to less able children, sometimes one feels as a form of therapy as much as for its educational value.

However, children of all ages and abilities enjoy and obtain value from making things, and if they can be offered the chance to design an object other skills can be trained and utilised. Learning is made easier for all children by their coming into contact with tangible evidence, in the form either of actual remains or of models, and it is one of the sad snobberies of history teaching that these activities are considered suitable only for the less literate child.

Models in the classroom can be roughly placed into three categories. Firstly, there are the demonstration models that a teacher might make to illustrate a class lesson – the battlefield of Balaclava; a Roman villa; a medieval village. Secondly, there are the commercial models that children can make from kits – Airfix or Solarbo for instance. Thirdly, there are the models that children can construct from their own designs and from simple materials obtainable in schools; wood, balsa wood, cardboard, plasticine and clay are the most easily worked materials.

There is added value if children can understand something of how archaeologists and historians work. For instance, one teacher deliberately broke an old vase and asked his pupils to restore the article as they might put together a jigsaw. Another form of modelling can be taken from one of the many suggestions made in the magazine *Pictorial Education* (monthly; Evans Brothers, Montague House, Russell Square, London, W.C.1), which has, as one of its features, a series of cut-out parts for a large model. The paper cut-outs have to be stuck to cardboard and fitted to make a large model. Some of the titles that have been offered in the past are: London Bridge, a Greek theatre and the Globe.

Materials

Model-making is not an end in itself. Construction is only half the purpose. In designing, making and painting objects, children are communicating and expressing themselves far more effectively than they could ever do in words. Moreover, when it is completed the model might be a classroom tool, either for demonstration purposes by the teacher or as part of a class display.

More sophisticated materials are now appearing on the market but the basic tools remain largely unchanged.

Plasticine : The advantage of modelling in plasticine is that the materials may be used again and again. Furthermore, plasticine can be used as binding and can be painted.

Cardboard and Wood : Cornflakes packets and cartons made from light cardboard are widely used in schools. Sheets of cardboard can be purchased from the normal educational suppliers. Plywood, hardboard, balsa wood and pegboard can be used for models and can be obtained from Do-It-Yourself, Hobbies or model-making shops. Other materials suitable for larger models are polystyrene sheets, corrugated card, dowelling, Plaster of Paris, Vinamold and chipboard. Polystyrene is an easily worked substance which is useful for walls, ceilings and almost any large surfaces; it can be painted with emulsion paint or poster paints.

Paints : Children gain as much enjoyment from painting their models as they do from constructing them. One needs a supply of some of the following: poster paints (sold by most artists' suppliers and by the ESA), powder paint, glues (including Copydex and clear Bostik); felt-tip pens; crayons; pens; pencils; inks; pastes and gums; cleaning, protecting and edging materials and some tools – scissors, penknives and, for more advanced work, saws.

Paper : a supply of paper of varying textures and thicknesses should be available: cartridge paper; sugar paper; newspaper; glass paper; wallpaper; ceiling papers and coloured sticky papers.

Fabrics : Fabrics suitable for cloth pictures are wool, crepe, cotton, hessian, felt, sacking, Dorset drape (for flannelgraphs), and buttons and sequins for decoration. Most of these fabrics can be obtained at a draper's shop. Cloth pictures are made by drawing the outline of the picture on a large sheet of paper. Figures are cut out from cloth and the pieces are stuck to the outline figures in the picture. Different colours and fabrics can be used to vary the effect.

Children's models

E. and E. K. Milliken, in *Handwork Methods in the Teaching of History*, describe in detail and with many illustrations how to make some forty or so models on subjects from prehistoric times, and from ancient, medieval and Tudor history. Their suggestions include hill-forts, a lake dwelling, a temple, a chariot, a Greek theatre and house, a Viking longship, castles, a tournament ground, a medieval monastery, a windmill and an Elizabethan playhouse. The instructions are easy to follow and from experience one can confidently assert that children both enjoy and gain value from making these models. The book is directed towards secondary school teachers.

The ideas put forward in *Art & Craft in Education* are largely planned for primary school teachers, but many of the schemes are suitable for secondary schools. The emphasis in the articles in this magazine is on child-centred learning, in which pupils explore materials and ideas for themselves instead of working to a rigid plan. John Fairley, in *Activity Methods in History*, describes a large number of ingenious models that can be made by primary school children from simple materials.

The term 'modelling' can mean something very elaborate or something very simple. Perhaps the easiest form of model is the stand-up figure made from cardboard, with tabs at the bottom and sides so that the object – a Roman soldier, a Tudor house front or Stephenson's *Rocket* – stands erect. Clothes for the figure can be made from sticky paper, pieces of wool and fur and silver paper (for armour). An effective backcloth for the figures can be made from cardboard. Another simple construction is the Peep-show, made from cardboard shoe boxes, with a hole pierced at one end to look through and a scene painted at the other. In the middle distance figures and objects can be drawn, cut out and mounted by means of tabs.

Models of buildings and vehicles are more sophisticated structures, but they can be made in a variety of ways from cardboard boxes of different shapes and sizes. A Viking homestead, for instance, can be made from a box covered with paper painted to resemble logs, and with grass glued to the roof to resemble turf. A Viking longship can be made from a wooden base, plasticine, sticks and paper or from a strong piece of card, balsa wood and dowel rod. Shields are made from cardboard and paper fasteners; the oars and mast are of dowel rod and the sails of cartridge paper. Glue, emulsion paint and varnish complete the construction. A Tudor shop

Collage 'Henry V' made by a boy aged 10 years from a linen background, leather pieces and various materials
By courtesy of Miss Eugenie Alexander and *Art and Craft in Education*

is made from three cardboard boxes of varying sizes, covered with strips of sticky paper and coloured with crayons. A motte and bailey castle can be made from a wooden base, balsa wood, foam rubber, cardboard and sticky paper. A trebuchet is assembled from wood and string.[1]

Models of trains, ships, aeroplanes and cars are more difficult, but again it is possible to achieve accuracy with simple materials. An early train can be made from corrugated paper (for the

barrel), with cardboard wheels, sides and funnel.

Relief models are rather like a map in three dimensions. Relief is obtained by using a large sheet of hardboard or plywood as a base, with paper, crushed chicken wire, papier mâché, sponge or foam rubber moulded into the shapes of mountains and valleys. A piece of hessian is glued or nailed over the relief features. Rivers can be painted on the hessian and towns, woods, armies or ships can be added. Silver foil serves as rivers, a handmirror as a lake, and corrugated paper as ploughed fields. Tents can be made from cones of paper. The relief model can serve as a battlefield – Waterloo, Quebec or Blenheim – or

[1] Note *Model Making as an Approach to Local History in the Middle School* by E. Happer and Joan E. Blyth in *Teaching History*, Vol. 1 No. 3, 1970.

Collage 'A Bishop' made by a boy aged 10 years from material stitched to a linen background
By courtesy of Miss Eugenie Alexander and *Art and Craft in Education*

it can show a Roman road system, open field farming or an industrial town in the nineteenth century. Miniature toy soldiers can be purchased to demonstrate the development of a battle.

Work-cards

The advantage of work-cards over more formal work patterns is that pupils can set their own pace to suit their ability levels. The able pupils can push ahead to complete a large number of assignments, whilst the slow learner has time to think and act without losing himself in the pursuit of more able fellows. There are various examples of work-cards contained within the pages of this book. They require patience to construct, but they have many educational advantages and are useful in that they can be used year after year. At the primary level, some of the *Ladybird* series have cards attached to them, but there are few other forms of this type of teaching aid on the commercial market.

In devising work-cards, one should set tasks of varying difficulty:

Information : One question, linked to a picture of Richard I, might simply ask children to find out details of his life and his part in the Third Crusade.
Imaginative reconstruction : Children can be asked to imagine themselves a medieval farmer, an eyewitness at Trafalgar, a newspaper reporter at Peterloo, or take the role of Marco Polo or Columbus. In various ways they can be asked to describe and explain their actions.
Interpretation of a picture : pictures from *Pictorial Education* or from a book such as *Evidence in Pictures* (Longmans) can be linked to work-cards.
Expression : Children can be set painting, drawing, modelling and sketching to illustrate their ideas on an event – Napoleon in Russia; building the Pyramids; the Roman army; and so on.
Judgements : Two differing accounts of the same event can be set side by side, or children can be asked to make judgements based on some written evidence.
Cartoons : Cartoons such as those by Rowlandson can be used to illustrate an event, and children can be asked to make their own cartoons, in strip form using pinhead figures, in the form of a Bayeux Tapestry mural or as plain drawings. As a variation on the usual sort of question: 'Write an essay on the Peasants' Revolt', one can ask children to: 'Draw pictures with footnotes illustrating the course of the Peasants' Revolt'.
Maps : Maps can be used in many ways; for instance:
(i) 'Draw a map to illustrate Napoleon's campaigns in Egypt.'
(ii) 'On an outline map of Britain, shade in the areas held by Parliament and the Royalists in 1643. Mark in the major battlefields of the Civil War.'

Individual work-card used with pupils of 11-14.

The picture on page 88 shows Queen Marie-Antoinette of France pleading for her life before the Revolutionary Tribunal.
1. Read an account of the French Revolution from 1789 to 1793 in your textbook or library book.
2. Answer these questions:
   (i) What punishment was imposed on the Queen and her husband, Louis XVI?
   (ii) Marie-Antoinette was very unpopular in France before the Revolution. Why?
   (iii) Which other famous men and women of the French Revolution were tried by the Revolutionary Tribunal?
3. Write out a newspaper report, with headlines, describing the trial. Give some details, such as the charge brought against the Queen, and the verdict.

In devising work-cards, the teacher should try to make them as attractive as possible. Questions can be mounted on pieces of cardboard of different colours and perhaps enclosed in a small envelope. Directions on the card should be simple and direct: the questions should also be clearly within the child's ability. Cards should be kept within reach in an easily accessible place – in a box or enclosed in a cloth packet pinned to the wall.

Written work

Note-taking and note-making have enjoyed a secure place in the study of history for too long. Most junior pupils make bad notes that are of very little use, simply because they cannot distinguish the relevant from the irrelevant, or because they see no point in the operation and therefore give the whole boring business very little of their attention. Consequently, the exasperated teacher falls back on dictated notes, a method of teaching history which has as little to

Marie Antoinette before the tribunal
By courtesy Archives photographiques Paris

Photograph by courtesy of Service Commercial Monuments
Historiques, Paris.

commend it as 'reading around the class'. If notes are thought to be absolutely necessary, surely one can duplicate a sheet, distribute it to the class, and then proceed with the real task of teaching.

Essay writing is another difficult and skilled exercise and should be used as a method of written work only in moderation. Ultimately one hopes that children will progress to the writing of polished prose, and this can only be accomplished with practice; but for the majority of children, except for those classes preparing for Ordinary level and Advanced level examinations, formal essay writing is merely an exercise in copying chunks of ill-digested factual material from books. Ideally, one wants teachers to devise means of recording, analysing and expressing information. If this can be done by means of more imaginative and varied methods than note-making and essays, why not give it a try? Pupils who are found to be incapable of composing essays can very often produce imaginative writing which surprises teachers in its depth of feeling and response to the past. One can ask for newspaper accounts, headlines, diaries, letters, broadsheets and cartoons rather than a straight essay.

One would also like to see children expressing their views and recording information in a number of ways. One can approach this by presenting pupils with a small group of documents or extracts connected to a theme. For instance, if one were tracing the history of transport in the 19th century, the teacher might have a number of contemporary accounts, a photocopy of a turnpike record (a ticket, advertisement and map), a picture of a mail coach and an account of a journey from a novel such as *Tom Brown's Schooldays* or *Nicholas Nickleby*. Using these materials, pupils can be set specific tasks – describing improvements in road building; analysing the effects for the towns and traders; writing stories and eye-witness accounts about highwaymen and coaching inns; writing obituaries or newspaper accounts of the work of Thomas Telford and I. K. Brunel; plotting routes on a map; drawing and painting pictures of travellers, towns, inns and other illustrations.

Illustrations

There are three documents on pages 90-92 which could be 'starters' for a scheme of work on transport in the 19th century. The documents, which all deal with travel by road, are:

1. An extract from *Tom Brown's Schooldays* by Thomas Hughes.
2. A picture of a busy changing post at Gloucester.
3. An advertisement from Griffith's *History of Cheltenham*, 1838.

The children's work that could be set on these documents might be arranged as follows:

Tom Brown's Schooldays
1. What were the pleasures for Tom Brown of riding by coach to school at Rugby?
2. Draw or paint a picture to illustrate this extract from the book. Try to find a copy of the book and read the rest of the story.

The scene at the Gloucester Hotel and Coffee House in 1828.
One coach (the Poole and Exeter) is loading up with mails brought from the Post Office to the coaches by carts.
1. In this picture there are a number of different vehicles. Find out the names of these vehicles.
2. Draw or paint a picture of a mail coach being raided by a highwayman.
3. What are the occupations of the shopkeepers shown in this picture? Why should Joseph Miller be proud to have his business associated with 'Billingsgate'?

The advertisement for Tanner and Bayliss
1. How long did it take waggons to travel from Gloucester to London and return? What were the difficulties that the drivers faced on this journey? How long would it take a lorry to travel from Gloucester to London and back today?
2. What are the differences between 'fly waggons', 'fly vans' and mail coaches?
3. Write a short story, illustrated by drawings, of a journey from Bristol to London. Draw a map to show the route.

Further activities
Make a scrapbook about transport by road in the 18th and 19th centuries.
Write two or three sentences about each of the following: turnpikes; tolls; General Wade; John Macadam; Thomas Telford.

Similar schemes could easily be devised for railways, canals, shipping and other aspects of transport. Children then build up a picture of travel in the past through their own efforts and by studying a number of different sources.

The Gloucester coffee house 1828
By courtesy of the Post Office

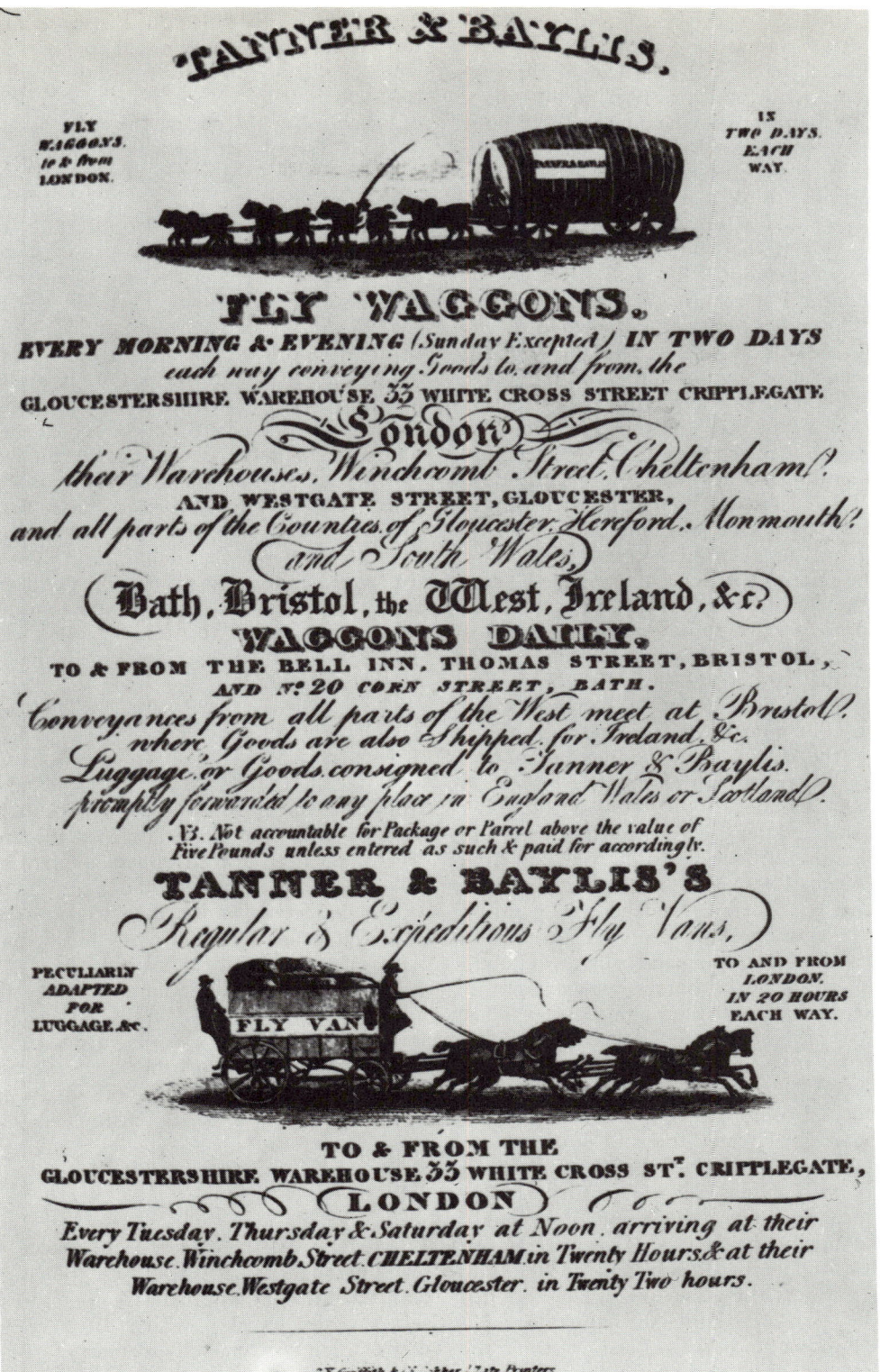

Advertisement from 'Griffith's History of Cheltenham and its Vicinity 1838'

'Tom stands up on the coach and looks back at his father's figure as long as he can see it; and then the guard, having disposed of his luggage, comes to an anchor, and finishes his buttonings and other preparations for facing the three hours before dawn – no joke for those who minded cold, on a fast coach in November.

I sometimes think that you boys of this generation are a deal tenderer fellows than we used to be. . . . It was another affair altogether, a dark ride on the top of the Tallyho, I can tell you, in a tight Petersham coat, and your feet dangling six inches from the floor. Then you knew what cold was, and what it was to be without legs, for not a bit of feeling had you in them after the first half-hour. But it had its pleasures, the old dark ride. First, there was the consciousness of silent endurance, so dear to every Englishman – of standing out against something, and not giving in. Then there was the music of the rattling harness, and the ring of the horses' feet on the hard road, and the glare of the two bright lamps through the steaming hoar frost, over the leaders' ears, into the darkness; and the cheery toot of the guard's horn, to warn some drowsy pikeman or the hostler at the next change; and the looking forward to daylight. . . . The Tallyho is past St. Albans, and Tom is enjoying the ride, though half-frozen. The guard, who is alone with him at the back of the coach, is silent, but has muffled Tom's feet up in straw and put the end of an oat-sack over his knees. . . . And now the dawn breaks at the end of the fourth stage, and the coach pulls up at a little roadside inn with huge stables behind. There is a bright fire gleaming through the red curtains of the bar window, and the door is open. The coachman catches his whip into a double thong, and throws it to the hostler; the steam of the horses rises straight up into the air. He has put them along over the last two miles, and is two minutes before his time. He rolls down from the box and into the inn. The guard rolls off behind. "Now, sir", says he to Tom, "you just jump down, and I'll give you a drop of something to keep the cold out".

In the bar . . . a fresh-looking barmaid serves them each with a glass of early purl as they stand before the fire, coachman and guard exchanging business remarks. The purl warms the cockles of Tom's heart, and makes him cough. . . . Soon they are out again and up; coachee the last, gathering the reins into his hands and talking to Jem the hostler about the mare's shoulder, and then swinging himself up on to the box—the horses dashing off into a canter before he falls into his seat. Toot-Toot-tootle-too goes the horn, and away they are again, five and thirty miles on their road (nearly half-way to Rugby, thinks Tom) and the prospect of breakfast at the end of the stage.

. . . "Twenty minutes here, gentlemen" says the coachman as they pull up at half-past seven at the inn door.

Have we not endured nobly this morning? And is not this a worthy reward for much endurance? There is the low, dark wainscoted room hung with sporting prints; the hat-stand (with a whip or two standing up in it belonging to bagmen who are still snug in bed) by the door; the blazing fire, with the quaint old glass over the mantelpiece, in which is stuck a large card with the list of the meets for the week of the country hounds; the table covered with the whitest of cloths and of china, and bearing a pigeon-pie, ham, round of cold boiled beef cut from a mammoth ox, and the great loaf of household bread on a wooden trencher. And here comes in the stout head waiter, puffing under a tray of hot viands, kidneys and a steak, transparent rashers and poached eggs, buttered toast and muffins, coffee and tea, all smoking hot. The table can never hold it all.'[1]

Workbooks

Children can make their own workbooks out of unlined sheets of paper, two cardboard covers (cereal packets, for instance) and sticky paper. The workbook is the record of a pupil's 'research' and a collection of his individual assignments, and if it is constructed from basic materials it will reflect the child's individuality. A brightly coloured cover, designed and made by the pupil, adds to enjoyment. The book can contain information sheets, poems, drawings, photographs, completed worksheets or questionnaires, maps, paintings, reports of visits, museum postcards and newspaper cuttings.

Drama

Dramatic work has great educational value in teaching history. In the first place, it gives children another opportunity to express themselves orally – a skill which often comes more easily than written self-expression. By placing themselves in the situations in which real people

[1] From *Tom Brown's Schooldays* by Thomas Hughes.

in the past found themselves, children can appreciate their views and understand something of their actions. Dramatic work might take the following forms:

(i) At its simplest, dramatisation can be miming to an extract read aloud in class. From this it is an easy step to impromptu dialogue, with a narrator on the side-lines. Dialogue should be spontaneous, because a set script may be difficult to learn and may inhibit self-expression. The roles in the playlet can be exchanged so that the same scene might be acted more than once, with additional impromptu material added as the children progress.

(ii) Dramatic work can also be expressed through making puppets, and by acting out a playlet with some children operating the puppets and others speaking the dialogue. Puppets can be made from papier mâché or more simply by drawing and painting figures on strong paper bags. Rod puppets can be made by sticking a face or head to a piece of stiff card which is sellotaped to a piece of wood or a school ruler.

(iii) A play that the class or a group of children have written and produce themselves is of great value. For instance, one has seen reconstructions of Henry II and Becket, a meeting of a manorial court, the coronation of William I and the trial of Warren Hastings.

(iv) A 'programme' similar to BBC broadcasts in which the children and the teacher write the script and record it on the tape-recorder is another form of dramatic interpretation.

One of the attractions of dramatic work lies in making the costumes. Children enjoy dressing up. Their imaginations are easily stirred by very simple ideas. Dressing gowns, belted adult coats and academic gowns can serve as medieval robes or Roman togas. A peasant's tunic can be made from cotton sheets or a sack with slits for head and arms, and with a rope at the waist. Cardboard sheets, fashioned and painted, can serve as armour. Helmets and ladies' hats can be constructed from stiff paper and old felt hats. One hopes that costume will be as accurate as possible, but it is after all only an aid to the drama, which is the chief activity, and therefore simple designs are all that are required for authenticity.

Scenery can be adapted from classroom furniture. The teacher's desk can serve as a castle or ship; desks can be arranged as houses in a town, or as barricades; clothes-horses are invaluable because they can be draped with painted paper, cotton sheets and hessian, and thus serve a dozen different purposes. Daggers, shields, lances and swords can be made from cardboard, broomstick handles and wood, and picnic paper plates and beakers (painted silver) resemble pewter plates.

Photo-play

Another effective approach to teaching history in a practical manner is through photo-play. This means that children tell their own story, in fictional or documentary form, of a historical event. A number of still photographs are arranged in a sequence, either as a filmstrip or as a set of slides, with the addition of a sound commentary, which is given orally or recorded on the tape-recorder. Again, this is not a particularly revolutionary idea: most people have at one time or another mounted photographs in an album, adding a title to each one. Yet it has rarely been adapted to history teaching. This method has the great advantage of flexibility and a wide range of practical activities can be drawn from the idea.

Equipment need not be expensive. An 'Instamatic' camera and a roll of black and white or colour film is sufficient for class use. Standards of photography need not be high: children are keen critics of their own work and will seek to improve the quality of the photography and the commentary on their own terms.

For the history teacher, photo-play can be used in a number of ways:

(i) As a documentary – recording an event (the procession of judges at an assize or a school trip abroad); or as a record of a class visit to a ruined abbey or castle; or in the form of a series of pictures on a theme such as local churches or the buildings of the town.

(ii) A fictional account of a story from the past. The children write a script, act it out and film it, after a number of rehearsals.

(iii) A filmstrip or slides illustrating some topic in local history: transport (canals, railways, roads); architecture or inn signs.

Music adds a great deal to the aural impact of photo-play and can be used as background material or as links in a story. Comments on the documentary or filmstrip should be made by children: it is a good idea to aim at a blend of dialogue and commentary, music and sound effects, so that the sound impact is as impressive as the visual one.

In fictional stories the children ought to do

some preparatory work. Actions and locations have to be decided and the script written. For the latter it is probably better to put it into the hands of a small group of the more literate youngsters, while others collect or make costumes and prepare any 'sets' or 'props' that might be needed. Story lines should be simple and contain plenty of dialogue.

One must expect a high degree of failure with one's first attempts. Children will make mistakes and much of the material will have to be jettisoned. However, if the teacher keeps the stories and the topics simple and concentrates all the action around one place (a church or a castle) or around an event, the technique has real educational value. Powers of imagination and observation are likely to be developed and the skills that children master are in themselves likely to be of use outside school.

References

Bell J. J., *History in School*, Wheaton, 1945

Casciani J. W., and Watt I., *Drama in the Primary School*, Nelson, 1966

Dean J., *Art and Craft in the Primary School*, Black, 1961

Fairley J. A., *Activity Methods in History*, Nelson, 1967

Francombe A., *Photo-Play*, Kodak Ltd

I.A.A.M., *The Teaching of History*, CUP, 3rd edition, 1966

Milliken E. and E. K., *Handwork Methods in the Teaching of History*, Wheaton, revised edition, 1960

Pluckrose H., *Let's Work Large*, Mills and Boon, 1967

Pluckrose H., *Let's Make Pictures,* Mills and Boon, 1964

Snook B., *Costume for School Plays*, Batsford, 1965

Snook B., *Puppets*, Batsford, 1965

Models

Airfix Products, Haldane Place, London, S.W.18

Britains Ltd., 184 King's Cross Road, London, W.C.1

Educational Models, 4 Avenue Road, Duffield, Derbyshire

Randall Page, 11 Old Bond Street, London, W.1

Solarbo Ltd., Commerce Way, Lancing, Sussex

Index